Carolina

RECIPES FROM THE REGION'S BEST CHEFS

Cooking

Carolina
RECIPES FROM THE REGION'S BEST CHEFS
Cooking

Written by Debra Zumstein & Wil Kazary
With Thom Zelenka and Aris Ragouzeos

Photography by Debra Zumstein

Gibbs Smith, Publisher
TO ENRICH AND INSPIRE HUMANKIND
Salt Lake City | Charleston | Santa Fe | Santa Barbara

First Edition
11 10 09 08 07   5 4 3 2 1

Published by
Gibbs Smith, Publisher
P.O. Box 667
Layton, Utah 84041

Orders: 1.800.835.4993
www.gibbs-smith.com

Designed by Dawn DeVries Sokol
Printed and bound in China

Library of Congress Cataloging-in-Publication Data
Zumstein, Debra.
  Carolina cooking recipes from the region's best chefs / written by Debra Zumstein and Wil Kazary, with Thom Zelenka and Aris Ragouzeos ; photography by Debra Zumstein. — 1st ed.
      p. cm.
  ISBN-13: 978-1-4236-0203-3
  ISBN-10: 1-4236-0203-X
  1. Cookery, American—Southern style. 2. Cookery—South Carolina. 3. Cookery—North Carolina. 4. Restaurants—North Carolina. 5. Restaurants—South Carolina. I. Kazary, Wil. II. Title.

TX715.2.S68Z95 2007
641.5975—dc22
                              2007011255

Contents

Introduction

Thanks for reading our cookbook. As I write this, I am trying to picture what you must be doing at this moment. Either you're the type of person who reads everything from page one or you are sitting in the bookstore with a cup of coffee, killing time and trying to decide if you want to buy this book. If it is the latter, do so. It's well worth it. The recipes are delicious and brilliant. But know that they are merely starting points. Experiment with them. Combine them. Swap out red onions with green onions. See what a difference that makes. Add more oregano than we said. Try basil instead. Use these recipes as a foundation and leapfrog off of them.

Wow. You're still reading! I'm flattered. At this point, I wonder if you're a fan of the TV show this book is based on. Maybe you want to know personal, behind-the-scenes stuff about the cast and crew. Maybe you're thinking of being a stalker . . . cool! There is part of me that thinks having a stalker legitimizes my TV presence. And there is another part of me that is kind of scared that you might want to know: Is Thom really as big a goofball in person? Is Aris as hot in person as he is on camera? Does the crew really attack the plate of food at the end of the show, like hyenas on a gazelle?

Well, here is some stuff you may not know about us:

First and foremost, our TV series, *Carolina Cooking,* is about having fun. Cooking is fun. Eating is fun. If you were to come to a party at my home, we wouldn't be hanging out in the living room; my rowdy friends and I would all be crammed into my steamy, smoke-filled, cramped chaotic kitchen. What is Carolina Cooking? It IS that kitchen.

The thing you rarely get to see is what really happens at the end of an episode. I say, "And that's Carolina Cooking." The cameras zoom and fly. Then the director booms out, "We're clear." The drawer of forks and spoons is opened. The whole crew gathers around the plates of food. We don't bother getting separate plates. We just stand in a circle, digging in, tasting, laughing and chatting, joking and teasing, complimenting the chef, questioning the chef . . . Could you do this with chicken? What if you don't have fresh basil? Where can you get this kind of rice? . . . oohing and aahing until even the garnish has been consumed.

Behind the Scenes on *Carolina Cooking*

We are a family. We eat together. We live together. We laugh together. We yell at each other. We fight with and for each other. We support one another. We have young ones and more mature ones and a very immature one who is really the oldest one. His name is Aris. We share in our victories and our defeats. And as cliché as it sounds for folks on a show to say, we love one another.

Debra runs Camera Two, the one that catches my enormous cranium from the side. She is the "mom" of the group and the whip cracker. Plus, she is the one that takes the beautiful photographs you see in this cookbook and on www.CarolinaCooking.TV. If you need to know what is going on at any given moment, she knows.

Wil is the Dad. He fixes what breaks, he directs the show and punches the buttons to change the camera shots you see. The show is his baby. He is always thinking of fourteen things at one time, but will always listen to a crazy idea I have and promptly say, "Yeaaahhhh . . . but why does it need to catch fire?"

Mikey is the kid. He is on Camera One, the one that flies down from the lights and roof. He loves *Star Wars* and we pick on him about his geekiness all the time. We are all very bad influences on him. He finds nothing I do funny or, if he does, he is unwilling to let me know. It is payback for all the guff I give him.

Bryan is the one whom we put on a pedestal—Camera Four. He is always looking down on us. His job is to get close-ups of the food or our hands from above. You forget he is there and then I say something ridiculous and I hear a guffaw from above. He is also the tallest. So any dangerous job that requires someone to stand on tippy toe, on top of a ladder to attach something to the ceiling, is his job.

Speaking of ladders, perched atop a little step-ladder so she can see into Camera Three is Lizzie. She is wee in height (5'0"), but huge in spirit. She is our Curly Sue—feisty, ornery and not to be underestimated. She is willing to whip any of us boys at our own game. When help is needed Liz is the first to offer a hand.

And Kristin, with her brilliant blue eyes and blonde hair, is the voice in my head. You see, while on camera I have an earpiece in my ear. The voice in that earpiece is Kristin. She and Wil, the director, talk to me, telling me how much time we have, and what we need to do next, and that I need to stand closer to the chef, stand up straighter, which camera to look into, smile, straighten my apron, fix my hair, and to stop looking like my mother is fussing over me. It is a nonstop monologue that I wish everyone could be privy to. The chefs don't hear a word and always stare at me curiously when I begin answering questions that they never heard anyone ask. It always weirds them out first thing in the morning. By the end of the day, they are used to my schizophrenia.

Aris, the wine guy, is the oldest member of the team. Somehow he has managed to exist in a world of wine tasting, spit buckets and "finishes with a hint of white asparagus," and not become a pretentious ass. If you've ever spent an afternoon in a high-end wine shop or vineyard, you can appreciate how hard that is for him to do. The wine he chooses for us meets an important criteria of being affordable and tasting good. He fully believes that good wine can be inexpensive. We love Aris, and that love has nothing to do with the cases of wine that accompany him. Honest.

Every chef brings extra ingredients just in case something goes wrong. Usually, they don't care to take those extras home with them. So, in the evenings, off the set, the cast and crew eat together. We are not required to be together after the shows, but we choose to make one more meal (our fourth) together. It is chaos. It is food experimentation at its best and worst. We take everything we have learned from the chef that very day and express it in new and dangerous ways. We create flavor combinations so rare and extreme that starving people would say, "No, thank you." But occasionally—actually more often than not—we make something pretty darn good. And believe me when I tell you, it is impossible to screw-up sushi . . . we tried . . . really hard . . . it can't be done.

I can truly say from all of us at *Carolina Cooking,* we hope the recipes in this cookbook inspire as many good times and great memories as they have for us.

—**Thom Zelenka**
Host of *Carolina Cooking*

Wine Makes
a Difference

Being the wine expert on *Carolina Cooking* has become one of the most interesting chapters of my life. Having spent most of my life as an analytical chemist dealing with computers and chemicals, I never dreamt at some point I would be found in front of a TV camera talking about wine.

What exactly is my job? I like to think that I find a harmony with the foods our guest chefs create and the perfect wine. With so many thousands of wines available, it may sound like an impossible job. Well, it takes a little experience getting to know the wines, just like a chef needs to learn about the spices and other ingredients used in cooking. But anyone who has done any creative cooking can learn how to match food and wine.

Being of Greek heritage and raised in a mostly Italian neighborhood, wine was a natural part of everyday life. These were not gourmet wines consumed from crystal stemware, but jugs taken from the fridge and poured unceremoniously into tumblers at meals. My involvement in wine as a serious hobby began in 1975 when I rewarded myself for quitting smoking with a case of expensive wine from a specialty store. The consultant at the store invited me to join his wine group that met at a local restaurant once a month to taste fine wine with equally fine food. Well, it's thirty years later and I'm still hooked.

What I'm hooked on is not just great wine but how it relates to food, which is a topic that surprisingly few cooking shows give more

than a passing reference to. Wine is, after all, a food. Wine is made from an agricultural product—grapes. I truly believe nature intended the juice from those grapes to be wine, because the yeast that converts the sugar into alcohol grows on their skins. The combination of a wine's alcohol and acidity give it a biological stability that inhibits the growth of most bacteria that are harmful to humans and keeps the wine stable for many years. After all, how many of you would drink a bottle of water that lay in someone's damp basement for twenty years? A bottle of Cabernet from the same basement will have you salivating.

The art of matching food and wine is easier if you think of the wine as a sauce being served with the dish. Wine, like any sauce, has flavor, body and texture. Although matching flavors is subjective, you do not want the wine's weight, flavor concentration or structure to overwhelm or clash with the dish, nor should you allow the dish to clash with or smother the wine. Once you learn about the various wines and what they offer, the wine rack takes its place beside the spice rack as another tool in your kitchen.

Since experience is your number one tool, how do you get it? Start at a specialty store where education and advice are their prime directives. Go to wine tastings, especially the free ones available at many specialty stores.

Here is a method I know will work. Let's say you drink four bottles of wine per week with dinner. Open all four at once. With each meal try a little of all four, regardless of how strange the match might sound. You will likely discover a few bad combinations and some matches made in heaven, but the wide majority will range from adequate to sensational. In no time at all, you'll be the wine-food guru people come to for advice.

When it comes to wine and food the learning process never stops. Carolina Cooking has given me the opportunity to try so many new and interesting wine-food combinations. We hope this book will get you started on your own journey into wine with food. The journey is a long one, but a blast every step of the way.

—Aris Ragouzeos
Wine Expert, *Carolina Cooking*

Appetizers

Stuffed Tomato with Mediterranean Couscous and Champagne-Tomato Butter Sauce

From: Four Square Restaurant • 2701 Chapel Hill Road • Durham, NC 27707

4 large, ripe tomatoes

1 cup couscous

1 cup water

1 tablespoon butter, cubed

½ teaspoon salt

1 tablespoon cooking oil

6 Spanish queen olives, sliced

6 kalamata olives, sliced

¼ cup diced red onion

1 clove garlic, minced

1 tablespoon capers

¼ cup diced red bell pepper, roasted

¼ cup diced yellow bell pepper, roasted

salt and pepper to taste

1 tablespoon basil, thinly sliced lengthwise

2 green onions, chopped

1 tablespoon minced chives

1 tablespoon minced parsley

1 tablespoon walnut oil

2 lemons, juiced

2 cups champagne

2 bay leaves

½ teaspoon whole black peppercorns

½ pound butter

Makes 4 servings

Preheat an oven to 400 degrees F.

In a large bowl, prepare an ice bath.

Cut out the top core and score an "X" in the bottom of each tomato with a paring knife. Place the tomatoes in 1 quart of rapidly boiling water. Boil for approximately 1 minute. Immediately remove to the ice bath. When cooled down, remove from ice bath. Peel away the skin. Cut the tops off the tomatoes and scoop out the rest of the core, the seeds and the pulp (do not discard). Slice the bottoms of the tomatoes so they will sit flat.

Put the couscous in a medium-sized mixing bowl. Bring 1 cup water, 1 tablespoon butter and ½ teaspoon salt to a simmer. Pour the water over the couscous, cover completely and let stand at least 5 minutes. Heat the cooking oil in a sauté pan over high heat. Add the olives, onion, garlic, capers and roasted peppers and sweat over medium heat for 3 minutes. Season with salt and pepper. Add basil and green onions. Sweat for 1 minute. Fluff the couscous with a fork. Add the vegetable mixture to the couscous and toss together. Add 2 teaspoons of the chopped chives and parsley, walnut oil, juice of one lemon and salt and pepper to taste.

Place the core, seeds and pulp of the tomatoes into a 1-quart saucepot. Add the champagne, bay leaves and peppercorns. Turn the heat to high and reduce until almost no liquid is left. Reduce the heat to medium and slowly whisk in the butter until emulsified. Remove from heat and season with salt and pepper to taste and the juice of the remaining lemon. Strain sauce through a fine mesh sieve, pushing down on the tomatoes with a small ladle or spoon to extract all of the flavor.

Place the tomatoes on a roasting pan and fill each with the couscous. Heat in the oven for 3 minutes. Remove from the oven and place each tomato on a plate. Ladle sauce over the tomatoes and onto the plates. Sprinkle with the remaining chives and parsley.

Wine Pairing:
Austin Hope — Westside Red

Aris's Wine Notes: Austin Hope works wonders with Rhone Valley grapes. This dish screams out for just such a red wine. The lush fruit balances the acidity of the tomato and lemon while the olives and peppers accentuate the wine's spice. A great combo! Oh, by the way, this wine is delectable on its own as well.

Thom's Tips: Before *Carolina Cooking*, when I saw recipes that said "peel tomatoes," I always picked up my peeling tool and had mixed results and lots of the tomato parts. Now I know that peeled tomatoes actually means remove the skins by placing in hot water, then in ice water. It helps to score the bottom of the tomato with an X so that you have a place from which to start peeling the loosened skin.

Smoked Salmon and
Trout Cavier Pizzetta

From: Inn on Biltmore Estate • 1 Approach Road • Asheville, NC 28803

1 tablespoon sugar

2 cups all-purpose flour

½ teaspoon salt

2 tablespoons olive oil

¼ cup canola oil

2 to 3 cloves garlic, minced

1 tablespoon dry yeast

1 cup warm water

Cocktail Reception Topping

¼ cup cream cheese

2 teaspoons chopped dill

8 to 10 slices smoked salmon

2 tablespoons trout caviar

Makes 4 to 5 pizzettas

Thom's Tips: You can spend your kids' college funds buying smoked salmon in 4-ounce packages. Or you can go to the deli section at your local grocery store and find nova lox that you can buy by the pound. It is not quite as pricey, but it is just as tasty.

Start your grill.

In a mixing bowl, using the dough hook attachment, combine sugar, flour, salt, oils and garlic. Add the yeast. Turn the mixer on slow speed. Slowly add water starting with half a cup. Add the remaining water a little at a time until fully incorporated and the dough pulls away from the side of the bowl. Continue to mix on low to medium speed for 3 to 4 minutes. Transfer to a large bowl and cover with a clean dry towel and proof for 8 to 10 minutes, or until it expands to twice the volume. Punch down the dough and proof one more time until it doubles again. Punch down again and divide the dough into 4 balls.

Turn your grill to high (allow 10 to 15 minutes for the grill to get hot). Meanwhile, lay one portion of the dough on a flat, lightly oiled pan. (I like to use the backside of a large pie pan or baking sheet.) Press the dough down and gently form into a circle. Once the dough is formed turn your pan upside down so the dough sits flat on your grill and cook for 1 to 2 minutes. Remove the pan. Flip the dough over and cook the other side.

Cocktail Reception Topping: In a bowl, soften the cream cheese and add dill. Spread the cream cheese on the pizzetta and top with smoked salmon and trout caviar.

Wine Pairing:
Biltmore Estate —— Methode Champenoise —— Blanc de Blanc Brut

Aris's Wine Notes: This is a perfect choice for this dish. The wine's acidity cuts through the oiliness of the salmon while the toasty/yeasty flavors complement the smokiness of the salmon and the fruit blends nicely with the fish flavors. In the end, those tiny scrubbing bubbles cleanse the palate and prepare you for another bite of the pizzetta.

Ceviche

From: La Cava Restaurant • 329 South Church Street • Salisbury, NC 28144

In a bowl, add the shrimp, lime juice and a pinch of salt and put into the refrigerator overnight.

The next day drain the shrimp and put into a bowl. Add tomato, onion, avocado and cilantro. Season with salt and red pepper. Drizzle extra virgin olive oil over the top and then plate.

Beer Pairing:
Copperline Amber Ale —Carolina Brewery

Aris's Beer Notes: The Copperline Amber Ale is a nice balance between malty richness and fruitiness of the ale yeasts, augmented by the tangy aroma and mouth-cleansing bitterness of the hops. Ceviche is too tart with acidity for most wines, but the Copperline ale balances it nicely, allowing its flavors to blend with the cilantro for a most interesting finish.

1 cup baby shrimp, peeled
¼ cup lime juice
salt
3 tablespoons diced tomato
3 tablespoons diced onion
3 tablespoons diced avocado
1 teaspoon chopped cilantro
crushed red pepper
extra virgin olive oil

Makes 4 servings

Thom's Tips: Ceviche is a dish in which the acid in the lime juice cooks the seafood. It's basically a chemical burn. Make sure the seafood is fully covered by the lime juice when you put it in the refrigerator overnight. You don't want any ends sticking out of the juice because they will stay uncooked.

Shrimp Tortuga with Grilled Pineapple–Black Bean Salsa

From: The Speedway Club • Lowe's Motor Speedway • PO Box 600 • Concord, NC 28027

8 16/20 count fresh shrimp, peeled

1 jalapeño

1 green bell pepper

4 slices apple-smoked bacon

¼ fresh pineapple, skin removed,
    cut into ¼-inch slices

salt and white pepper

½ red onion

½ red bell pepper

1 (12-ounce) can black beans

2 cups chopped fresh cilantro,
    divided

⅛ cup sweetened lime juice

½ cup canola oil

cooking oil

micro cilantro

Makes 4 servings

Thom's Tips: When butterflying shrimp, first peel the shell from the shrimp. This will give you much more control over the depth of your paring knife and will leave you with a better chance of keeping your fingers attached. You don't need to devein the shrimp before you butterfly them, because you are cutting right along the back of the shrimp. Just make sure you wash the shrimp when you are finished.

Butterfly the shrimp (see Thom's Tips) and set aside.

Slice the jalapeño and bell pepper. Remove the seeds from both peppers. Set aside half of the bell pepper. Mince the jalapeño and half of the bell pepper very fine. Stuff this mixture inside the shrimp. Wrap the stuffed shrimp with half of a bacon slice. Secure with 2 wooden toothpicks.

Season the pineapple slices with salt and white pepper. Grill on both sides. Once grilled, dice the red onion, remaining bell peppers and pineapple. Combine these ingredients with the black beans and toss with ¼ cup chopped cilantro and the sweetened lime juice. Adjust the seasonings with salt and pepper.

Purée the remaining cilantro in a blender with the canola oil and strain through cheesecloth. Set the cilantro oil aside.

Fry the shrimp in a deep fryer until golden brown. Place a spoonful of the salsa in the center of the plate with two bacon-wrapped shrimp intertwined with one another on top. Drizzle a little cilantro oil around the outside of the dish and place a small bundle of micro cilantro on top of the shrimp to garnish.

Wine Pairing:
Falling Star — Sauvignon Blanc

Aris's Wine Notes: Sauvignon Blanc with shellfish and/or vegetables is a no-brainer. Falling Star, from Argentina, blends the softer and fruitier Semillon grapes to polish off the rough edges of the tart Sauvignon Blanc. They produce a new quality wine for a really low price.

Asian Tapas
—Dumplings

From: JuJube Restaurant—Asian Kitchen and Bar • 1201-L Raleigh Road • Chapel Hill, NC 27514

Pork and Shrimp Dumplings

¼ pound shrimp, chopped in chunks
1 pound ground pork
1 cup diced shiitake mushrooms
½ cup chopped garlic
½ tablespoon cornstarch
¼ cup Shaoxing cooking wine
salt, pepper and sugar to taste
1 tablespoon sesame oil
wonton skins

Pan-Fried Pork & Cabbage Dumplings

½ pound ground pork
½ cup finely chopped Napa cabbage
½ tablespoon chopped garlic
½ tablespoon chopped ginger
1 tablespoon sesame oil
salt and pepper to taste
wonton skins
oil for frying

Pickled Cucumbers

1 English cucumber, thinly sliced
2 teaspoons fish sauce
2 teaspoons sweet chili
2 teaspoons rice vinegar
1 tablespoon chopped cilantro
1 tablespoon chopped fresh mint
squeeze of lime juice

Makes 6 servings

Pork and Shrimp Dumplings: Mix together all ingredients except wontons. Place 1 tablespoon of the filling in middle of the wontons. Gather up sides around filling to create an open-faced dumpling, pinching at the top. Repeat until you've used all the filling. Steam in an oiled dim sum steamer basket or similar configuration for approximately 3 minutes. The dumplings should feel quite firm when poked.

Pan-Fried Pork and Cabbage Dumplings: Mix together all ingredients except wontons. Place 1 tablespoon of filling in the middle of the wontons. Form into cockscomb shapes. Brush water along wonton edges; fold in half and pinch edges together firmly. Repeat until you've used all the filling. Cook in boiling salted water for 2 minutes and drain. In a nonstick pan large enough to hold dumplings in one uncrowded layer, pan-fry dumplings in about 1 teaspoon oil per dumpling until browned on all sides. Add more oil if pan becomes dry.

Pickled Cucumbers: In a bowl, combine sliced cucumbers, fish sauce, sweet chili, rice vinegar, cilantro, mint and a squeeze of lime. Stir and set aside.

Serve the dumplings on a plate with a side of pickled cucumbers.

Aris's Wine Notes: Euroa Creek Shiraz gets its extraordinary depth from its low-yielding vines. Swirling reveals a thick and opaque wine that bursts forth with dark fruit flavors of blackberry and plum with a rich mocha overlay and spicy notes of vanilla, mint and black pepper. The flavors seem to linger forever. Wow, this is Shiraz at its best.

Thom's Tips: When mixing ground meats, such as ground pork for dumplings or ground beef for a meatloaf, there is just no substitute for kneading the meat and spices with your hands. Make sure you wash your hands before and after you touch the meat.

Creole Barbecued
Shrimp

From: Fenwick's On Providence • 511 Providence Road • Charlotte, NC 28207

Homemade Creole Seasoning

2 tablespoons cayenne pepper

2 tablespoons black pepper

2 tablespoons paprika

1 teaspoon dried thyme

1 teaspoon dried oregano

1 teaspoon onion powder

1 teaspoon garlic powder

1 cup butter

½ cup olive oil

4 tablespoons minced garlic

juice of 2 large lemons

1 cup white wine

2 tablespoons Worcestershire sauce

2 to 4 tablespoons Homemade
   Creole Seasoning (see recipe)

1 tablespoon dried basil

5 tablespoons black pepper

4 teaspoons salt

2 pounds large fresh shrimp,
   shells on

* OPTIONAL:

dash of hot sauce

lemon pepper seasoning to taste

Makes 4 to 6 servings

Thom's Tips: I like hot food. In fact, I like hot food so much I sometimes overdo it. To douse the heat I drink milk. It works every time.

Mix all Homemade Creole Seasoning ingredients and set aside.

In a large skillet melt the butter in the olive oil. Add garlic, lemon juice, wine, Worcestershire sauce, Homemade Creole Seasoning, basil, pepper, salt and optional hot sauce and lemon pepper. When butter is melted, seasonings are incorporated and sauce is hot and bubbling, add shrimp and cook until completely pink, stirring often.

Pour into serving dish or serve straight from the skillet with lightly toasted French bread for dipping.

NOTE: This is an easy dish for entertaining. You can prepare the sauce hours ahead, then cook the shrimp in a few minutes. If your guests love shrimp, figure about $1/4$ pound per person. The recipe easily doubles.

Wine Pairing:
Dashe — Zinfandel

Aris's Wine Notes: Dry Creek Valley Zinfandels are amongst California's finest and this Dashe is a great ambassador for the region and the grape. I rarely pair reds with shellfish but feel that the ripe fruit will absorb the Creole spices, creating a new sauce for the shrimp. It worked as well as any red could, but I think I'll return to a German Riesling the next time.

Savory Crepes with Lobster

From: 700 Drayton—Mansion on Forsyth Park • 700 Drayton Street • Savannah, GA 31401

Preheat oven to 350 degrees F.

In a mixing bowl, combine eggs, milk, water, flour, butter, salt and fresh herbs. Whisk well. Place the crepe batter in the refrigerator for 1 hour. This allows the bubbles to subside.

Heat a small non-stick pan and add butter to coat. Pour ¼ cup of the batter in the center of the pan. Swirl to spread evenly. Cook for approximately 30 seconds; flip. Cook for another 10 seconds; remove and lay flat then allow to cool. After cooled they can be stacked with wax paper between the layers.

Savory Crepe Filling: In a bowl, mix the lobster, fennel, salt and pepper. In a saucepan, heat the heavy cream. Add lobster and fennel and cook until tender. Spoon filling onto crepe. Fold and roll crepe. Heat in oven until warm; do not overcook.

Plate and garnish with sour cream and caviar.

Wine Pairing:
Neveu ——Sancerre 'Clos des Bouffants'

Aris's Wine Notes: This wine shows why Sancerre is often called the Chablis of the Loire. The nose is penetrating and the palate fresh and racy with steely acidity. The solid core of fruit shows excellent density and length, being lean and svelte rather than ripe and round. It's hard to imagine a better wine with these Savory Crepes with Lobster

2 large eggs
¾ cup milk
½ cup water
1 cup flour
3 tablespoons melted butter
¼ teaspoon salt
¼ cup freshly chopped herbs,
     spinach or sun-dried tomatoes
butter for coating the pan

Savory Crepe Filling
¾ cup lobster, cooked and diced
fennel bulb, diced
salt and pepper to taste
½ cup heavy cream
sour cream for garnish
caviar for garnish

Makes 4 servings

Thom's Tips: Leftover crepe batter can be stored in the refrigerator for up to 2 days. By simply changing the filling ingredients, I am able to enjoy crepes for breakfast, lunch and dinner.

Shrimp and Prosciutto Spedini with Tomato Basil Vinaigrette

From: Gianni & Gaitano's • **14460-171 New Falls of the Neuse Road** • **Raleigh, NC 27614**

12 16/20 count shrimp, peeled and
    deveined, tails-on

12 thin slices prosciutto, cut in
    2-inch strips

3 (10-inch) wood skewers, soaked
    in warm water

1 tomato

4 tablespoons olive oil, plus extra
    for seasoning tomato

kosher salt

¼ teaspoon chopped garlic

¼ teaspoon chopped shallot

1 teaspoon chopped basil

2 tablespoons red wine vinegar

2 handfuls baby greens

Makes 4 servings

Thom's Tips: If using wooden skewers, remember to soak them in water overnight. That way when you fill them with food and place them on the grill they don't catch fire. This imparts the flavor of the spedini without losing your food in the grill.

Preheat oven to 350 degrees F.

Wrap each shrimp with prosciutto and slide 4 onto each skewer. Grill skewers 2 minutes on each side until prosciutto is crispy.

Core tomato and cut an X in the bottom. Season with olive oil and kosher salt. Roast in the oven for 5 minutes. Peel tomato skin. Put tomato in food processor with the garlic, shallot, basil and vinegar. Process until smooth, then drizzle in the 4 tablespoons of olive oil.

Set greens on middle of a plate. Remove shrimp from skewers and arrange evenly around the greens. Drizzle with the tomato vinaigrette.

Wine Pairing:
Franciscan Oakville Estate — Chardonnay

Aris's Wine Notes: This Franciscan Chardonnay is classically Napa Valley in its broad stroke of ripe apple, citrus and tropical fruits. The texture is creamy, yet there is plenty of acidity to give a firm backbone. It does not overwhelm the shrimp, but makes it taste like you added a rich butter sauce. The oak was a nice match for the smoky, meaty prosciutto.

Tuna
Canapé

From: Chelsea's Wine Bar & Eatery • **One South Front Street** • **Wilmington, NC 28401**

Preheat oven to 375 degrees F.

Quarter the tomatoes and toss with the herbs, garlic, oil, and a pinch of salt and black pepper. Place on a baking sheet, cut side up, and bake until semi dry, approximately 20 minutes. Remove from oven. Remove tomato skins. Chop tomatoes and put aside.

Slice baguette into ¼-inch slices and season with oil and a pinch of salt and black pepper. Toast until crisp, but not brown.

For the red pepper jus, coat peppers with oil. Grill the peppers until the skin is completely blackened and blistered. Transfer peppers to a bowl and cover with plastic to finish cooking. Once cooled, peel and seed the peppers. Purée the peppers in a food processor until creamy. Strain through a fine mesh strainer, then season the jus with a pinch of salt.

Fire your grill.

Season the tuna on both sides with oil and a pinch of salt and black pepper. Grill all sides over high heat until rare. Slice the tuna to fit the baguette slices.

Chiffonier the spinach, and refrigerate until assembly.

Top the toasted bread with the thinly sliced tuna, then the chopped roasted tomatoes. Next add the spinach, and dress the bruschettas with the red pepper jus and olive oil.

Wine Pairing:
Etude —Pinot Noir Rosé

Aris's Wine Notes: Etude makes one of California's best Pinot Noirs. The color is a bright salmon and the nose and palate are filled with strawberry, rose petal and pomegranate. The match with the tuna is near perfection, providing red wine flavors with white wine refreshment.

5 Roma tomatoes

2 sprigs rosemary, minced

3 sprigs thyme, minced

1 tablespoon garlic, minced

½ cup olive oil, plus ¼ cup for tomatoes

1 tablespoon salt

1 tablespoon black pepper

1 baguette

2 red bell peppers

16 ounce yellowfin tuna steak

1 cup baby spinach

Makes 4 servings

Thom's Tips: Grilled red peppers are easy to make. Just place the pepper directly on the gas burner of your stove. Leave it there until the skin is bubbled, black and nasty looking. You can do the same on a grill or in the broiler if you have an electric oven. Let the peppers cool and peel off the black skins. Or you can do it the really easy way and buy roasted red peppers at the store. But the chefs say that's cheating.

Oysters
Rockefeller

From: Vinnie's Steakhouse & Seafood • 7440 Six Forks Road • Raleigh, NC 27615

12 fresh oysters on the half shell

4 tablespoons sambuca

12 tablespoons Creamed Spinach (see recipe)

12 tablespoons Hollandaise (see recipe)

Hollandaise

3½ cups butter

5 egg yolks

½ lemon, juiced

¼ cup white wine

⅛ cup water

Dash white pepper

Dash garlic salt

Dash Worcestershire sauce

Dash Tabasco sauce

Creamed Spinach

1 pound fresh spinach, finely chopped

⅓ quart half-and-half

¼ cup grated Pecorino Romano cheese

Pinch black pepper

Pinch salt

Pinch garlic salt

Roux thickener (1 cup flour and ⅔ cup melted butter)

Makes 4 servings

Drizzle oysters with sambuca. Cook oysters under broiler for 5 to 10 minutes, depending on the size of your oysters. Remove from oven. Top with Creamed Spinach and Hollandaise. Return to broiler. Broil until lightly brown.

Hollandaise:

Melt butter in pot. Add yolks to mixing bowl. With whisk, slowly add hot butter, whisking continually. Do not add too much butter at one time or the sauce will break. When sauce reaches a thick consistency, slowly add lemon juice, wine, water, pepper, garlic salt, Worcestershire and Tabasco.

CAUTION: Whisk this sauce continually so as to not break or separate sauce!

Creamed Spinach:

Put spinach in a pot. Add half-and-half and heat slowly. Add cheese and spices. Cook over medium heat for 15 minutes then whisk in roux to thicken.

Wine Pairing:

Robert Mondavi— Stags Leap District Sauvignon Blanc

Aris's Wine Notes: From a single vineyard in the Stags Leap AVA, one of Napa's best sub-regions, this wine makes a dramatic statement. Using lots that were barrel fermented and barrel aged helps hold the classic herbaceous, lemongrass flavors in check while adding richness and complexity to the intense pear and melon fruit and mineral notes.

Thom's Tips: Opening raw oysters is a tough job. I have been outsmarted many times by the mollusk. Use your knife to leverage open the shell by placing the blade about 10 degrees away from where the two shells are connected, the hinge. Twist and the shells should pop open. It is also a good idea to hold the oyster in a dish towel; in case the knife slips, you hit the towel and not your hand.

Fiery Shrimp Tostadas— Tostadas de Camaron a la Diabla

From: The Prickly Pear • 761 North Main Street • Mooresville, NC 28115

10 to 15 Chile de Arbol peppers

1 tablespoon canola oil

4 medium Roma tomatoes, quartered

4 cloves garlic, divided

1 whole clove

10 peppercorns

1 tablespoon butter

12 medium-sized shrimp, peeled and deveined

kosher salt

ground black pepper

2 tomatoes, diced

2 tablespoons finely chopped yellow onion

1 teaspoon chopped cilantro

1 lime, juiced

1 avocado

4 corn tostadas

Makes 4 servings

Thom's Tips: Here's a simple tip to getting the pit out of the avocado without turning your avocado into mush. First, cut the avocado in half from top to bottom. Then, take the sharp heel of your knife and with one strike stick it into the pit of the avocado. When the knife is stuck in the pit, twist the knife and the pit should pop right out.

Toast the Chile de Arbol peppers in a sauté pan with canola oil over medium heat until fragrant and slightly darker. Remove peppers to a plate. Reserve oil for sautéing shrimp.

Purée Roma tomatoes, 3 cloves garlic, clove, peppercorns and peppers in a food processor or blender; strain mixture into a bowl.

Finely chop the remaining clove of garlic and place in sauté pan with reserved oil over medium heat. Let the garlic caramelize. Add butter and melt. Add tomato mixture to sauté pan and bring to a simmer, stirring occasionally. Add shrimp and cook for about 4 to 5 minutes. Add salt and pepper to taste.

Combine diced tomato, onion and cilantro in a small mixing bowl. Add lime juice and toss ingredients. Add salt and pepper to taste.

Cut 8 slices of avocado and then place 2 slices on each tostada. Place 2 shrimp on each tostada and a teaspoon of sauce. Top off each tostada with a tablespoon of the Pico de Gallo.

Wine Pairing:
Greg Norman—Victoria Chardonnay

Aris's Wine Notes: The spice, heat and tomatoes in the dish call for either a mildly sweet wine or a dry wine with enough ripe fruit and creamy texture that it acts like a sweet wine to balance the ingredients. I choose the lush, dry style here, and this Greg Norman Chardonnay performs admirably.

Bruschettas

From: San Francisco Oven • 7223 North Kings Highway • Myrtle Beach, SC 29572

Traditional Tomato Bruschetta

6 to 8 Roma tomatoes

1 medium red onion

5 leaves fresh basil, chiffonade cut

1 teaspoon salt

1 teaspoon pepper

1 loaf Italian, French or focaccia
   bread, cut in ¾-inch slices

½ cup grated fresh Romano cheese

1 tablespoon extra virgin olive oil

Shrimp & Escarole Bruschetta

1 tablespoon extra virgin olive oil

1 cup finely diced raw shrimp

1 cup diced Roma tomatoes

¼ cup diced garlic

1 head escarole, chopped

1 teaspoon salt

1 teaspoon pepper

1 loaf Italian, French or focaccia
   bread, cut into 3/4-inch slices

1 cup grated fresh Romano cheese

Wild Mushroom & Prosciutto Bruschetta

1 tablespoon extra virgin olive oil

½ cup wild mushrooms

1 teaspoon minced garlic

¼ cup thinly sliced prosciutto ham

1 tablespoon toasted pine nuts

1 teaspoon chopped fresh oregano

Traditional Tomato Bruschetta:

Cut tomatoes in half and scrape seeds out with a spoon. Cut to medium dice. Peel and dice red onion. Add to tomatoes with basil, salt and pepper; chill.

Toast bread in broiler. Spoon tomato mixture on bread. Top with Romano cheese. Drizzle with olive oil and serve.

Shrimp & Escarole Bruschetta:

Heat oil in large sauté pan over medium heat. Add shrimp and quickly sauté until 70 percent cooked. Add tomatoes, garlic and escarole to shrimp. Sauté 1 to 2 minutes, being careful not to brown garlic; strain liquid and then add salt and pepper. Reserve mixture.

Lightly toast bread in broiler. Spoon shrimp mixture on bread. Top with Romano cheese. Place under broiler for 1 to 2 minutes. Serve warm.

Wild Mushroom & Prosciutto Bruschetta:

In a large sauté pan, heat oil over medium heat. Add mushrooms, garlic, prosciutto and pine nuts. Cook until mushrooms are tender, approximately 3 minutes. Add oregano, salt and pepper and sauté for 30 seconds. Reserve mixture.

Lightly toast bread in broiler. Spoon mushroom mixture on bread. Top with mozzarella cheese. Place under broiler 1 to 2 minutes. Serve warm.

Wine Pairing:
Ravenswood — Amador 'Old Vine' Zinfandel

Aris's Wine Notes: Ravenswood's Amador Zinfandel is the most distinctive Zinfandel grown in California, marked by a trademark cocoa-cherry quality with chewy tannins and aromatic spices. The complex flavors and firm acidity gave this wine the flexibility to handle these bruschettas, although the match with the shrimp was the least successful.

1 teaspoon salt
1 teaspoon black pepper
1 loaf Italian, French or focaccia bread cut in ¾-inch slices
1 cup grated mozzarella cheese

Makes 6 servings

Thom's Tips: Fixing bruschetta is a great way to clean out the refrigerator. Mix and match vegetables and meats. Dice them up small. Place on toasted bread that has been rubbed with garlic. Voila! Amazing appetizers.

Chorizo and Fennel
Empanadas

From: Chelsea's Wine Bar & Eatery • One South Front Street • Wilmington, NC 28401

1 cup melted butter

1 shallot, minced

⅓ bulb fennel, small dice

2 cups chorizo, skinned
   and crumbled

1 egg

1 tablespoon minced tarragon

1 tablespoon chopped chives

½ cup grated manchego cheese

1 cup breadcrumbs

salt and pepper

1 sheet puff pastry, thawed

Cream Sauce

½ pound unsalted butter, softened

1½ cups sour cream

½ cup cream cheese

1 teaspoon salt

Red Pepper Vinaigrette

1 (14-ounce) can fire-roasted red
   bell peppers

1 cup champagne vinegar

1 teaspoon granulated garlic

1 teaspoon dry thyme

½ teaspoon crushed red chili flakes

1½ cups olive oil

salt and pepper

Makes 6 servings

Preheat the oven to 425 degrees F.

Heat a sauté pan over medium heat and then add the butter. Add the shallot and sauté until tender. Add the fennel and cook until softened. Remove the shallot/fennel mixture to a cooling pan. Add the chorizo to the sauté pan and cook, rendering all the fat. Drain the chorizo and cool completely. Mix the shallot and fennel with the cooled chorizo. Add the egg, tarragon, chives and manchego. Fold in the breadcrumbs until all ingredients are thoroughly mixed. Season with salt and pepper.

Cut the puff pastry into 8 equal slices and divide the mix among the slices equally, leaving ½ inch on both ends to pinch closed. Roll the pastry over the mix, sealing the empanada at the ends and the crease. Place the empanadas on a baking sheet and bake in the oven for about 8 minutes. Turn them over and continue to bake until golden brown for another 4 minutes. Take the empanadas out of the oven and cut into thirds. Serve with the Cream Sauce and Red Pepper Vinaigrette.

Cream Sauce: Place the butter, sour cream, cream cheese and salt in a mixer with a whisk attachment. Whip until all blended and smooth.

Red Pepper Vinaigrette: Roughly chop the peppers and place in a food processor. Add the vinegar, garlic, thyme and chili flakes; process until smooth. Slowly add the oil until completely emulsified. Adjust seasonings with salt and pepper to taste.

<u>Wine Pairing:</u>
McManis — Petite Sirah

Aris's Wine Notes: McManis is notable for producing wines for the value-conscious consumer. This Petite Sirah is just what the doctor prescribes. Although rich and full bodied, it has a smooth and rounded finish with very little astringency. The spicy chorizo sausage and licorice notes from the fennel marry well with the ripe berry and pepper-spiced fruit, as do the cheese and red peppers.

Thom's Tips: I've become a big fan of empanadas because you can put just about anything in them. Need to clean out the fridge? Make empanadas. Chicken and bleu cheese? Tastes great. Salmon and bacon? Yummy. Baking soda and ice chips? O.K.; you've reached the back of the fridge. Go to the store.

Gambas al Ajillo—
Garlic Shrimp with Sherry

From: Gervais and Vine • 620-A Gervais Street • Columbia, SC 29201

1 pound 31/40 count shrimp,
    peeled and deveined
1 tablespoon chili powder
1 tablespoon paprika
½ teaspoon cayenne pepper
1 teaspoon salt
6 tablespoons olive oil, divided
2 tablespoons minced garlic
½ cup diced tomato
3 slices, crispy prosciutto, broken
    into bits (optional)
1 cup dry sherry
chopped parsley
lemon wedges
1 cup diced manchego cheese
1 tablespoon thyme
2 teaspoons garlic

White Sangria

½ cup sugar
¼ cup water
1 fresh peach
1 bottle white wine (Spanish table
    wine like Vuira, Verdejo or a
    fruity Pinot Grigio)
½ cup Gran Marnier
1 cup orange juice
1 cup pineapple juice
Fresh peach, orange and apple slices

Makes 6 servings

In a mixing bowl, combine shrimp with chili powder, paprika, cayenne pepper and salt. In a sauté pan over medium-high heat, add 3 tablespoons olive oil. When hot, add shrimp and sauté until cooked halfway. Add garlic, tomato and prosciutto and sauté a bit longer. Add sherry and cook until reduced by half. Sprinkle with parsley and squeeze lemon wedges over the shrimp.

Toss manchego cheese with thyme, garlic and remaining olive oil. Serve shrimp with toasted slices of rustic bread and diced cheese.

White Sangria: Combine sugar and water in a small saucepan. Over medium heat, cook until sugar dissolves (this is simple syrup). Remove from heat and allow to cool.

Peel and pit peach and then purée in a blender. Combine all ingredients in a pitcher; stir to mix. Refrigerate at least 8 hours or up to 48 hours. Serve over ice.

Black-Eyed Pea Hummus with Corn Bread Sticks

From: 700 Drayton—Mansion on Forsyth Park • 700 Drayton Street • Savannah, GA 31401

Drain and rinse the peas. Place in a food processor, reserving ¼ cup. Add garlic, tahini and lemon juice and purée. Slowly add the olive oil, making sure to scrape down the sides of the bowl. Add ice and continue puréeing until the cubes are melted. Season with salt and pepper.

Place the ingredients in serving bowl. With the back of a spoon, make a channel in the center of the hummus. Drizzle with ¼ cup olive oil, remaining peas, parsley and paprika.

Corn Bread Sticks: Preheat oven to 300 degrees F. Mix all ingredients together except cheese and allow the batter to rest for 3 minutes. Place parchment paper on a sheet pan. Spray with non-stick cooking spray. Pour the batter into a disposable pastry bag. Pipe 8-inch sticks onto the parchment. Top with Parmesan cheese. Bake for 15 to 20 minutes or until golden brown. Allow to cool and then serve with the hummus.

Beer Pairing:
SweetWater 420 Pale Ale

Aris's Beer Notes: First brewed on 4/20/97, this lovely pale ale is SweetWater's most popular brew. I usually reserve the term's elegance and finesse for wine but they fit perfectly with this beer's personality. It is light and refreshing, yet full flavored and complex with a lovely balance of hops and malt. Be forewarned: the combination of this beer with this unique hummus will turn you into a couch potato.

1 (16 ounce) can black-eyed peas
2 cloves garlic
¼ cup tahini paste
juice of 1 lemon
½ cup extra virgin olive oil
½ cup ice
kosher salt and white pepper
¼ cup extra virgin olive oil
¼ bunch flat-leaf parsley
1 tablespoon Hungarian or sweet
   paprika

Corn Bread Sticks

1 box (8.5 ounce) Jiffy Corn
   Muffin Mix
1 whole egg
⅓ cup milk
1 teaspoon cornstarch
1 cup grated Parmesan cheese

Serves 4 to 6

Thom's Tips: Adding small amounts of ice when blending the hummus keeps the mixture from getting too hot, thus allowing the oil to mix in without separating. The result is a creamy and rich hummus.

Portobello Formaggio
with Balsamic Reduction

From: Gianni & Gaitano's • 14460-171 New Falls of the Neuse Road • Raleigh, NC 27614

½ cup balsamic vinegar

4 portobello mushrooms

½ cup mascarpone cheese

½ cup ricotta cheese

2 tablespoons grated Parmesan
   cheese

2 tablespoons chopped basil

salt and pepper

flour for dredging

2 large eggs beaten

¾ cup plain breadcrumbs

3 tablespoons extra virgin olive oil

3 handfuls baby arugula

Makes 4 servings

Thom's Tips: The portobello mushroom gills don't necessarily have a bad taste, but when you are cooking with portobello mushrooms, the gills will separate from the mushroom cap and give your food a dirty look. You will want to strip the gills out of the mushroom with the side of a spoon.

Preheat oven to 350 degrees F.

Pour balsamic vinegar in a small saucepan. Cook over medium heat until reduced to syrup. Do not stir.

Remove stems from mushrooms and scrape off gills with a tablespoon. Mix together cheeses and basil. Add salt and pepper to taste. Place a thin layer of cheese evenly on gill side of mushrooms. Dredge top side of mushroom in flour. Dip entire mushroom in eggs and coat with breadcrumbs. Oil a baking pan and place mushrooms cheese side up. Drizzle tops with olive oil. Bake for 10 minutes, or until mushrooms are tender.

Place arugula on four plates. Top with mushrooms. Drizzle with the balsamic reduction and more olive oil.

Wine Pairing:
Estancia — Meritage

Aris's Wine Notes: "Meritage" refers to a high-quality wine made from a blend of the Bordeaux grapes. This Estancia is a little more than half Merlot with Cabernet Sauvignon making up the rest and, boy, does it have a lot of class. It has all of the prerequisites necessary to handle the complexity of the portobellos, the richness of the cheese and the intensity of the balsamic.

Soups & Salads

Vidalia Onions and Potato Cheddar Cheese

From: Crescent Grill • 1035 Broad Street • Camden, SC 29020

¼ pound butter

1 head garlic, peeled and chopped

5 Vidalia onions, julienned

salt and pepper

1½ cups flour

8 cups chicken stock

5 Yukon gold potatoes, diced

1 quart heavy cream

4 cups grated cheddar cheese

½ pound bacon, for garnish

Makes 6 servings

Thom's Tips: For crispy bacon, stack bacon slices on top of each other. Cut in half and freeze. Once frozen, cut bacon into thin strips, then dice. Add bacon to sauté pan and render until crispy. Strain grease.

In a medium-size stockpot, melt butter. Add garlic and sauté for about 30 seconds. Add the onions and cook until translucent. Season with salt and pepper. Add flour to make a roux. Cook about 3 to 4 minutes, stirring constantly.

Add chicken stock to the stockpot. Add diced potatoes and bring to a boil. Cook until potatoes are soft. Add cream and cheese; stir constantly. Season to taste. Cook bacon until crispy. Crumble and add to soup for garnish.

Wine Pairing:

Wente —— Livermore Valley Cabernet Sauvignon

Aris's Wine Notes: This Cabernet Sauvignon proved to be an excellent match for this rich and flavorful soup, providing ripe plum and cherry fruit with notes of cedar and vanilla to match the richness of the cheese and sweetness of the onions. The texture of the wine also matched the texture of the dish, plush yet solid. Background notes of toasty oak played off the smoky notes of the bacon.

Chilled Avocado Soup
with Crab and Cilantro

From: Mangia Mangia • 100 State Street • Columbia, SC 29169

Sauté onion and garlic in olive oil.

Into a blender, add chicken stock, avocados and lime juice; purée. Add onions and garlic. Add cream and seasonings; purée and then chill. Correct seasoning as needed. Serve in a chilled bowl topped with a sprinkle of crabmeat and cilantro.

You aren't cooking the crabmeat in the soup, so for health concerns you will need to use either pasteurized or already cooked crabmeat as the soup topping.

Wine Pairing:
Murphy-Goode — Island Block Vineyard Chardonnay

Aris's Wine Notes: Delicious by itself or for the table where rich foods like this soup need taming. That Chardonnay will match with crab is a no-brainer, but the avocado's richness and the cilantro spice needed this wine's rich texture and firm structure for balance.

1 large onion, diced
3 cloves garlic, finely minced
3 tablespoons extra virgin olive oil
1 (14-ounce) can chicken stock
8 ripe avocados, peeled and pits removed
3 limes, juiced
1 pint whipping cream
2 teaspoons salt
1 teaspoon cayenne pepper
½ cup crabmeat, pasteurized
1 bunch cilantro, chopped

Makes 6 servings

Thom's Tips: This is a soup that will allow you to play with hot spices. The creaminess of the avocados and whipping cream helps calm the spices. If you like spicy, go wild and enjoy.

Blueberry Stilton
Spinach Salad

From: 45 South • 20 East Broad Street • Savannah, GA 31401

5 shallots

olive oil

1 cup white wine

3 sprigs thyme

4 cups spinach, stems removed

½ cup blueberries

8 endive spears

1 pear, julienned

3 tablespoons toasted pine nuts

½ cup crumbled Blueberry Stilton

Red Wine Citrus Vinaigrette

½ cup red wine vinegar

½ cup lemon juice

1 shallot, rough chop

1 tablespoon Dijon mustard

½ cup honey

2 cups olive oil

salt and pepper to taste

Makes 4 servings

Thom's Tips: From watching the show, I am sure you know that one of the things I love to do most is spend the 30 minutes whisking vigorously. There is an easier way. Take the ingredients for the vinaigrette. Place in a mason jar. Make sure that the lid is secured, now shake. It is a great way to make an emulsified salad dressing and while shaking you can start a congo line.

Place shallots in roasting pan coated in olive oil, 1 inch white wine and 3 sprigs of fresh thyme, cover with aluminum foil and roast until soft.

Toss spinach with blueberries, caramelized shallots and vinaigrette. Place atop endive spears. Top salad with pear, pine nuts and cheese.

Vinaigrette: Blend together red wine vinegar, lemon juice, shallot, mustard and honey. Slowly (very slowly or dressing will not emulsify) drizzle in olive oil in a thin steady stream until emulsified. Add salt and pepper to taste.

Wine Pairing:
Pedroncelli — F. Johnson Vineyard Pinot Noir

Aris's Wine Notes: Under most circumstances I would have picked a more robust, tannic wine to cut through the richness of the Stilton cheese. This dish, however, uses the tartness of red fruits to help provide balance, so a less tannic and more subtle Pinot Noir is needed. Spiced Bing cherries are the first impression, but plum and tart cranberry emerge as the wine airs.

North Carolina
Farmhouse Salad

From: Pewter Rose Bistro • 1820 South Boulevard • Charlotte, NC 28203

1 small zucchini, 1-inch slices

2 sweet red bell peppers, sliced

2 sweet green bell peppers,
1¼-inch slices

1 large red onion, 1¼-inch slices
(larger outer rings only)

2 Granny Smith apples, cored and
wedged into 8 pieces

3 tablespoons extra virgin olive oil

½ cup pecans

1 pound roast pork loin, thinly
sliced (or other available meat)

4 ounces goat cheese

Bacon Goat Cheese Dressing

8 ounces sour cream

1 teaspoon red wine vinegar

4 slices bacon, cooked crisp and
crumbled

1 tablespoon diced red onion

pinch black pepper and kosher salt

pinch cayenne pepper

pinch thyme, dry

2 ounces goat cheese

heavy cream, as needed

Makes 4 servings

Thom's Tips: It's so tempting to get a huge zucchini that you can use for a dugout canoe, but I truly believe that the smaller ones taste better. Also, most of the taste is in the skin.

Toss all vegetables and apples together with oil until lightly coated. Place in single layer on grill or under hot broiler. Cook, turning only once, to char each side and slightly soften. Remove to a bowl.

Toast the pecans in oven until fragrant and lightly browned; set aside.

Warm pork in oven or microwave. Toss vegetables with dressing until lightly coated. Top meat with vegetables. Crumble goat cheese on top of salad. Sprinkle toasted pecans over salad.

Bacon Goat Cheese Dressing: Add all ingredients to a blender and purée until smooth. Adjust consistency with cream.

Wine Pairing:

La Puerta — Shiraz

Aris's Wine Notes: I must admit to a preference for red wines with a ripe, jammy fruitiness as a match for pork. Having the goat cheese, bell peppers, tart apples and spices are added incentive to provide balance with a ripe and juicy red. La Puerta's Shiraz provides loads of spiced cherry fruit and a structure that is firmly tannic but not astringent.

Chicken Pecan Salad
with Pecan Vinaigrette

From: San Francisco Oven • **7223 North Kings Highway** • **Myrtle Beach, SC 29572**

Toss together all salad ingredients except chicken. Drizzle Pecan Vinaigrette over salad. Top with sliced breaded chicken and pita chips.

Pecan Vinaigrette: Place vinegar, honey, parsley and salt in a food processor and blend for 30 seconds. Add oil slowly and pulse processor until oil is incorporated. Stir in nuts and chill.

Wine Pairing:

Simi — Sauvignon Blanc

Aris's Wine Notes: I'm always wary about seeming predictable, but when it comes to salads with vinaigrette dressings I just gotta have Sauvignon Blanc. Simi can always be counted on to provide top of the line quality and value. This well-crafted Sauvignon Blanc has the bright, citrus acidity to balance the dressing, the herbaceous/grassy notes to complement the vegetables and the rich melon and fig fruit flavors to handle the chicken.

3 cups torn romaine lettuce

1 cup field greens

¼ cup diced tri-color peppers

½ cup diced tomato

¼ cup blue cheese crumbles

1 to 2 slices crisp bacon, crumbled

¼ cup grated cheddar cheese

¼ cup toasted pecan pieces

4 (6-ounce) chicken breasts, breaded, pre-cooked and cut in pieces

5 wheat pita chips

Pecan Vinaigrette

½ cup red wine vinegar

¼ cup honey

¼ cup chopped fresh parsley

1 tablespoon salt

½ cup extra virgin olive oil

½ cup vegetable oil

½ cup chopped toasted pecans

Makes 4 servings

Thom's Tips: If you want to toast your pecans, you do not need to oil the pan. They have plenty of oil already in them. Because of their high oil content they cook quickly.

Coriander Seared Scallops with Grapefruit Salad

From: Motor Supply Company Bistro • **920 Gervais Street** • **Columbia, SC 29209**

12 diver scallops (large dry-pack
    sea scallops)

salt and pepper to taste

4 tablespoons vegetable oil
    or butter

6 tablespoons sugar

4 tablespoons coriander

1 grapefruit, peeled and segmented

2 tablespoons extra virgin olive oil

baby greens

6 tablespoons goat cheese

1 tablespoon chopped fresh thyme

salt and pepper

Makes 4 servings

Thom's Tips: I do suggest getting a brulée torch. Not only can you use the torch for a number of dishes, it's also fun to play with such an implement of destruction. You can go to a fancy cooking supply store and pay about $40 for an elegant stainless steel, propane torch. Or, if you're like me, you can go to an auto parts store and buy a propane torch for about $12. It's bigger, easier to use and doesn't need to be refilled as often. Plus, when your cooking gear has NASCAR logos on 'em, you know you're Carolina Cooking.

Heat a heavy sauté pan. Season the scallops with salt and pepper. Sear scallops on both sides in a sauté pan with the vegetable oil or butter, flipping when golden brown. Turn off the pan.

If you have a torch, you can top the scallops with sugar and coriander and brulée them. This caramelizes the sugar and gives the scallops a sweeter taste. If you don't have a torch, just put the sugar and coriander on the scallops before you sear them.

Peel and segment the grapefruit. Squeeze the grapefruit core juices into a bowl. Toss the grapefruit juice with the grapefruit wedges, olive oil, greens, goat cheese, thyme and a pinch of salt and pepper.

Place salad and 3 scallops on each plate.

Wine Pairing:
Smoking Loon — Viognier

Aris's Wine Notes: The palate is ripe with apricot, peach and citrus, while the honeyed finish includes a kiss of clove spice. There are no oak flavors to interfere with the highly focused fruit and floral elements. This dish has an elegance and simplicity to it. It is not a simple dish, but rather subtle and charming. The wine is similar and works well.

Bavarian Potato Salad
with Red Onion
and Poppyseed Palmiers

From: 700 Cooking School—Mansion on Forsyth Park • 700 Drayton Street • Savannah, GA 31401

2 pounds red skinned potatoes, cut
    in 1-inch chunks

½ pound smoked bacon, cut in
    ¼-inch pieces

½ cup finely diced yellow onion

2½ teaspoons caraway seeds

¼ cup cider vinegar

¼ cup granulated sugar

¾ cup mayonnaise

½ teaspoon salt

1 Granny Smith apple, cored and
    diced ½ inch

1 cup shredded red cabbage

4 green onions, white and light
    green parts only, chopped

2 stalks celery, diced ¼ inch

Red Onion and
    Poppy Seed Palmiers

3 tablespoons butter

3 tablespoons olive oil

3 cups finely diced red onions

1 teaspoon kosher salt

3 tablespoons poppy seeds

½ teaspoon black pepper

1 sheet puff pastry

Makes 6 servings

Place potatoes in a large pot of heavily salted cold water over medium-high heat and bring to a boil. Simmer until potatoes can just be pierced with a paring knife. Drain and place into a non-reactive mixing bowl; set aside.

While potatoes are boiling, place bacon in a sauté pan and cook over medium heat until fat is rendered and bacon is crisp. Using a slotted spoon, remove bacon from sauté pan and drain on paper towels. Add diced onion and caraway seeds to bacon grease in sauté pan. Cook until onions are softened and caraway seeds are toasted. Carefully add vinegar to pan and stir in sugar. Cook until sugar is dissolved. Pour warm dressing over potatoes and place in refrigerator to chill.

Combine mayonnaise with salt, apples, cabbage, green onions and celery. When potatoes are cooled, pour mayonnaise mixture over top and then stir to blend. Garnish with cooked bacon and caraway seeds. Serve with Palmiers.

Red Onion and Poppy Seed Palmiers: In a sauté pan, heat butter and olive oil until the butter melts. Add diced red onions, kosher salt, poppy seeds and black pepper. Cook until red onions are soft and poppy seeds are toasted. When onions are soft and tender, remove from heat and cool to room temperature.

Preheat oven to 375 degrees F.

Place puff pastry on work surface so that the long side faces you. Spread half of the onion mixture over the top of the dough. Fold the long sides in to the center so that the edges meet. Spread remaining filling across top of dough and fold in half lengthwise. Roll across with rolling pin to flatten slightly. Cut into ½-inch cross-sections and place cut side up on a baking sheet. Bake for about 12 minutes. Remove from oven and cool.

Wine Pairing:

Jean-Baptiste Adam — Gewurztraminer Reserve

Aris's Wine Notes: Gewurztraminer is a hard wine to pair with food but it found real compatibility with this dish. You can use Gewurztraminer to match the spices in your dish or to add spice to a more neutral dish.

Thom's Tips: Because those extra hours allow the potatoes to absorb the flavors of the onions, spices and bacon, the flavor will be best if prepared a day in advance.

Summer Vegetable
Salad

From: North Beach Grill • Tybee Island, GA 31328

1 head Boston lettuce

2 ripe tomatoes

salt and pepper

2 ears corn

2 yellow squash

4 portobello mushrooms

2 zucchini

2 green onions

2 tablespoons olive oil

1 tablespoon chopped garlic

2 tablespoons chopped ginger

1 tablespoon diced shallots

snow peas

2 whole basil leaves

¼ cup sambuca or Pernod

2 tablespoons sesame seeds

Makes 4 servings

Thom's Tips: Don't let the "summer" in this recipe title fool you. With vegetables that you can find year round in your grocery store you can have a taste of summer in the dead of winter.

Wash and dry lettuce. Line serving dishes with several leaves of lettuce. Cut 2 medium slices from tomato and place on lettuce slightly overlapping one another. Lightly salt and pepper tomato slices.

Shave corn from cob. Julienne the squash, mushrooms and zucchini. Chop green onions.

In a large sauté pan, add 2 tablespoons olive oil and heat over high. Add garlic, ginger and shallots to pan. Follow with corn, squash, mushrooms, zucchini, green onions and snow peas. Add whole basil leaves. Toss vegetables quickly and often. Add sambuca and allow liquid to reduce. Add salt and pepper to taste.

In a small sauté pan, heat the sesame seeds. Do not add oil or other liquid. Allow seeds to toast until a golden color.

With tongs, place vegetable sauté on top of the lettuce and tomato. Top with toasted sesame seeds.

Wine Pairing:
Golding — Lenswood Sauvignon Blanc

Aris's Wine Notes: High in the Adelaide Hills region of South Australia the sun blesses the grapes with the warmth required to reach a delectable ripeness, but the cool nights allow the grapes to retain their crisp acidity. Sauvignon Blanc thrives in this climate, yielding this vibrant fruity wine, redolent of lime and passion fruit, with all the classic herbal, gooseberry and lemongrass aromas and flavors that marry so well with complex salads like this.

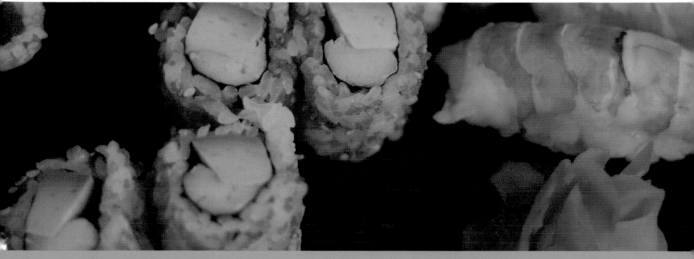

Sushi

Vegetarian
Sushi

From: Made in Japan Catering • PO Box 240724 • Charlotte, NC 28224-0724

2 cups sushi rice

2¾ cups water

¼ cup rice vinegar

1½ tablespoons sea salt

1½ tablespoons sugar

½ tablespoon mirin

Caterpillar and Cucumber Rolls

4 seaweed wrappers, cut in half

sesame seeds

½ carrot, julienned

½ apple, julienned

1 avocado, sliced

1 English cucumber

mixed greens

toasted pine nuts

Roasted Red Pepper Aïoli

3 tablespoons mayonnaise

1 tablespoon and 1 teaspoon garlic
    chili paste

¼ roasted red pepper

Tomato & Basil Nigiri

2 Roma tomatoes

2 basil leaves

½ cup balsamic vinegar, reduced by
    two-thirds

Pre-cook sushi rice with water according to package directions.

Mix rice vinegar and sea salt. Whisk until dissolved. Add sugar and whisk. Add mirin and whisk. Combine mixture with rice with a cutting motion. Try to not compress the rice.

Caterpillar Roll: Take a sushi roller covered in plastic. Place a seaweed sheet that has been cut in half on the roller. Dip your hands in water. Take some rice and spread it out on the seaweed. Don't squish the rice; keep it fluffy. Sprinkle sesame seeds on the rice. Flip the rice and seaweed over. Place julienned carrots and apples in the middle of the seaweed. Place your thumb on bottom of sushi roller. Roll the roller over the sushi and tightly compress the rice and vegetable roll. Remove the skin from half an avocado. Thinly slice the avocado. Slide the avocado out in your hand. Lay the avocado on the sushi roll. Take the sushi roller and press the avocado onto the roll. Slice the roll. Add drops of Roasted Red Pepper Aïoli (see below) to top of roll.

Roasted Red Pepper Aïoli: Blend together mayonnaise, garlic chili paste and roasted red pepper; set aside.

Cucumber Roll: Cut the cucumber into 4-inch pieces. Take the knife and, with your thumbs steadying the knife, peel the skin off in a circular motion, continuing into the meat of the cucumber. When you have enough cucumber to make a roll, cut the skin off. Julienne the skin. Set aside. Lay out the cucumber roll. Add rice. Sprinkle on sesame seeds. Add mixed greens, carrots, cucumbers, avocado slice and pine nuts. Drizzle on Wasabi Cilantro Cream. Fold like a waffle cone.

Wasabi Cilantro Cream: Whisk together sour cream, buttermilk, mayonnaise, cilantro, horseradish, wasabi, salt, pepper, lemon juice and garlic. Set aside.

Tomato & Basil Nigiri: Blanch Roma tomatoes in boiling water for 15 to 20 seconds. Remove from water. Drop in ice bath. Remove and peel off the skins. Slice in half and remove seeds. Place onto sushi rice ball. Press tomato and rice together. Top with chopped basil and balsamic reduction.

Wine Pairing:
Okunomatsu Sake

Aris's Wine Notes: What could be more natural than Japanese sushi with Japanese sake? Premium sake is brewed with special rice in which the desired starch component is concentrated at the center of the grain. This Okunomatsu is a junmai level sake, which means that about 30 percent of the outer portion of the grain has been milled away. The best sake will have 65 percent milling. Sake is best served lightly chilled. The aromas and flavors are very delicate and subtle, as is the texture.

Wasabi Cilantro Cream

2 cups sour cream
4 tablespoons buttermilk
4 tablespoons mayonnaise
½ bunch cilantro, chopped
½ teaspoon horseradish
½ teaspoon wasabi or wasabi paste
salt and pepper
1 teaspoon lemon juice
⅓ teaspoon minced garlic

Makes 4 to 6 servings

Thom's Tips: The 'sticky rice' lives up to its name. The water keeps the rice from sticking to your hands. I have learned the power of the clap. Spray water on your hands, then clap so that your palms make a pop. This will shake the excess water off of your fingers, but keeps just the right amount of water in your palms.

Ultimate Cold Sushi Nachos

From: Made in Japan Catering • **PO Box 240724** • **Charlotte, NC 28224-0724**

½ pound tuna, sashimi grade
1 large tomato, diced
Ponzu Vinaigrette (see recipe)
8 wonton skins, fried
1 avocado, diced
Wasabi Cilantro Cream (see recipe)
Roasted Red Pepper Aïoli (see recipe)

Wasabi Cilantro Cream

2 cups sour cream
4 tablespoons buttermilk
4 tablespoons mayonnaise
½ bunch cilantro, chopped
½ teaspoon horseradish
⅛ teaspoon minced garlic
½ teaspoon wasabi oil or paste
pinch salt and pepper
1 teaspoon lemon juice

Roasted Red Pepper Aïoli

3 tablespoons mayonnaise
1 tablespoon and 1 teaspoon garlic chili paste
¼ roasted red pepper

Ponzu Vinaigrette

½ cup ponzu vinegar
1 teaspoon garlic chili paste
black pepper to taste
lemon juice

Makes 4 Servings

Slice tuna against grain. Dice into bite-sized pieces. Add diced tomato to tuna. With half of the Ponzu Vinaigrette, wash tomato and tuna. This slightly cooks the tuna and gives added flavors.

Place wontons on a plate. Add tablespoons of tuna and tomato to wontons. Top with diced avocado. Drizzle Wasabi Cilantro Cream over top and place Roasted Red Pepper Aïoli on the side of the plate.

Wasabi Cilantro Cream:

Whisk together sour cream, buttermilk, mayonnaise, cilantro, horseradish, garlic, wasabi, salt, pepper and lemon juice; set aside.

Roasted Red Pepper Aïoli:

Blend together mayonnaise, garlic chili paste and roasted red pepper; set aside.

Ponzu Vinaigrette:

Whisk together ponzu vinegar, garlic chili, black pepper and lemon juice; set aside.

Wine Pairing:

St. Rita - Piesporter Michelsberg Riesling Kabinett

Aris's Wine Notes: German wine is an excellent match for so many oriental dishes, especially where there is heat, like the wasabi in this dish. This delightful Mosel has the delicacy to pair with the sashimi grade fish, the light sweetness to handle the wasabi and the acidity to cleanse the palate. Like so many good matches, both the dish and wine were improved by the new flavors and textures produced.

Thom's Tips: You can get sashimi-grade fish at most of your high-end local grocery stores. I usually ask if they can cut a piece from the supplies that they have in the back so that I don't run the risk that the sushi grade fish has been touched by lower grade fish in the display case. Often the fish cuts, especially the tuna, are still sealed in the shipping plastic when they are handed to me.

Shrimp Nigiri, Tuna Roll and California Roll

From: Made in Japan Catering • PO Box 240724 • Charlotte, NC 28224-0724

2 cups sushi rice

2¾ cups water

¼ cup rice vinegar

1½ tablespoons sea salt

1½ tablespoons sugar

½ tablespoon mirin

4 shrimp

4 skewers

¼ pound tuna, sashimi grade

seaweed wrappers

wasabi

2 tablespoons sesame seeds

½ cup Alaskan crab legs or fake crabmeat

1 avocado, sliced

Vinegar Shrimp Wash

¼ cup rice wine vinegar

1 tablespoon salt

1 tablespoon sugar

¼ cup rice cooking wine

½ cup water

Makes 4 to 6 servings

Thom's Tips: Remember to leave ¼ inch of the seaweed free from rice so that you can close your roll. Just moisten this lip of seaweed to adhere the roll shut. This works much like licking an envelope. I don't really suggest licking the seaweed though . . . you might have a lot of sushi that your guests won't want to eat.

Pre-cook sushi rice with water according to package directions. Mix rice vinegar and sea salt. Whisk until dissolved. Add sugar and whisk. Add mirin and whisk. Combine mixture with rice with a cutting motion. Try to not compress the rice.

Shrimp Nigiri: Skewer the shrimp by holding it flat. Slide through from head to tail; add to boiling salted water. Remove shrimp once it is orange. Add to ice water and cool; remove skewer. If the skewer is removed before the shrimp cools it will curl up. Peel shrimp, leaving tail attached, then butterfly and remove vein. Wash in Vinegar Shrimp Wash. Make rice ball. Place shrimp on top of rice and then press together.

Vinegar Shrimp Wash: Whisk vinegar and salt. Add sugar and cooking wine. Dilute with water; set aside.

Tuna Roll: Slice tuna against grain. Cut slice in half. Place seaweed wrapper shiny side down. Place rice onto wrapper. Spread rice to edge leaving a lip on one side. Spread wasabi onto rice. Lay tuna slices over top. Use bamboo roller to roll up. Cut roll into pieces. Keep knife moist when cutting rolls.

California Roll: Place rice on seaweed. Spread out over wrapper. Add sesame seeds to rice. Flip rice and wrapper over. Add pre-cooked crab legs and avocado. Roll up. (Remember to use a bamboo roller covered with plastic wrap when making rice on the outside rolls.) Slice and serve.

<u>Wine Pairing:</u>
Bonny Doon — Pacific Rim Dry Riesling

Aris's Wine Notes: This was an easy match because the wine is made specifically for this type of dish. The nose is a lovely blend of flowers and ripe fruits. Apples, grapefruit, apricots and lime blossom are a delight to the senses and blend effortlessly with the food. The refreshing acidity sets up the palate for another round of delights.

Pastas & Pizzas

Lobster Ravioli

From: Mia Famiglia • 19918 North Cove Road • Cornelius, NC 28031

1 pound chopped lobster meat,
  cooked and drained

1 egg

½ cup mascarpone cheese

½ cup goat cheese

4 large basil leaves, chiffonaded

1 teaspoon black pepper

½ teaspoon minced fresh garlic

½ teaspoon minced fresh thyme

salt to taste

5 fresh pasta sheets (see recipe
  below)

2 eggs, beaten

flour or cornmeal

Sherry Cream Sauce (see recipe
  below)

¼ cup grated Parmesan/Romano
  blend

Basic Dough

3½ cups all-purpose flour, sifted

4 large eggs

1 tablespoon extra virgin olive oil

flour

Sherry Cream Sauce

2 tablespoons extra virgin olive oil

2 tablespoons minced garlic

1 teaspoon salt

1 teaspoon black pepper

1 tablespoon chopped parsley

Mix together lobster meat, egg, cheeses, basil, pepper, garlic, thyme and a pinch of salt. Lay two pasta sheets on top of each other and cut into six equal squares. Separate the squares. Place one heaping tablespoon of the mixture in the center of half the pasta squares. Brush the edges of each sheet with egg wash (two beaten eggs) and cover the squares with the other six squares of pasta. Firmly press the edges together. Lay on a sheet pan lined with parchment paper that has been dusted with flour or cornmeal (cornmeal is better if available).

Cook until al dente in boiling, well-salted water.

Place 2 to 3 ravioli's on a plate. Cover with Sherry Cream Sauce and grated Parmesan/Romano cheese.

Basic Dough: Sift flour. Combine flour, eggs and olive oil in a mixer. Mix with dough hook attachment until combined. Place mixture on a flat surface dusted with flour. Knead the dough until completely combined. Wrap in plastic wrap and let rest in a refrigerator for at least 2 hours. Once dough has rested, divide the pasta dough into 5 to 6 balls. Roll out with rolling pin until it is thin enough to fit through pasta machine. Feed through pasta machine five times, lowering the setting on the machine one notch each pass through the machine. Cut off the rough edges, dust with flour, and lay out on parchment paper on a sheet tray.

Sherry Cream Sauce: In a cold pan, place olive oil, garlic, salt, pepper and parsley. Heat over high heat. Just as the garlic starts to golden, remove from heat and add sherry. Return to heat and reduce by half. Add cream and simmer over medium-low heat for 10 minutes. Cut butter into cubes and roll them in flour, dusting off the excess flour;

whisk the coated cubes into the sauce. Continue to stir until the butter is melted and the sauce has thickened slightly. Continue to simmer for 2 minutes and pour over the ravioli on a platter.

Wine Pairing:
Black Box — Chardonnay

Aris's Wine Notes: The Black Box motto is "think inside the box." There you will find a vacuum-sealed plastic bag filled with the equivalent of four bottles of wine. As wine is drawn from the spout the bag collapses, preventing air from entering and spoiling the wine. Black Box Chardonnay is a high-quality, classy wine with a delectable fruity character redolent of apple, pineapple and tropical fruits that provide the richness and body weight to match the dish.

½ cup pale sherry
1 quart heavy cream
½ stick butter
flour

Makes 4 to 6 servings

Thom's Tips: The main difference between the food I get at a gourmet restaurant and the food I make at home is not the level of difficulty in preparing the meal, but taking the time to start with the freshest food. A great meal starts, not in the kitchen, but at the grocery store and the farmers market. Chose wisely, pay more for the better quality of meat, get the ripest veggies you can find and cook them tonight.

Pea and Ricotta Ravioli
with Parmesan Cream

From: Frazier's Bistro • **2418 Hillsborough Street** • **Raleigh, NC 27607**

1 large onion, sliced thin

1 shallot, sliced thin

1 clove garlic, sliced thin

¼ cup mint leaves, picked, few reserved for garnish

½ cup pea shoots (tendrils), few reserved for garnish

1 pound frozen peas, blanched

¼ cup mascarpone cheese

1 cup ricotta cheese, drained

¼ cup grated Parmesan cheese

¼ cup breadcrumbs

drizzle of extra virgin olive oil

salt and pepper

1 cup heavy cream

½ cup grated Parmesan cheese, reserve some for garnish

4 leaves romaine lettuce, shredded

Ravioli Dough

¾ pound all-purpose flour

⅓ pound semolina flour

¾ tablespoons salt

½ tablespoon extra virgin olive oil

2 to 3 egg yolks

4 eggs

1 tablespoon water

Makes 4 to 6 servings

In a medium sauté pan over medium-high heat, sweat the onion, shallot and garlic until beginning to tender. Add mint and pea tendrils. Cook everything together until soft but not brown. Set aside until cool, then proceed. Purée the cooked ingredients with peas, cheeses and breadcrumbs in a food processor until smooth. Season with olive oil, salt and pepper. Strain the mixture through a cheesecloth or fine-mesh colander for several hours to thicken.

Bring the cream and Parmesan cheese to a simmer in a small pot. Simmer together until a nice, thick cream has formed (about 20 minutes); set aside.

Ravioli Dough: Combine flours and salt in the bowl of a standing mixer fitted with the dough hook attachment. Mix on low, then stream in olive oil, egg yolks, eggs and water. Continue mixing until dough is developed and elastic.

Run dough through a pasta attachment until desired thickness or roll out with a rolling pin. Lightly flour table and place dough on table. Cut two equally-sized pieces. Take the first piece of dough and place 1 tablespoon of filling every 3 inches. Cover with the 2nd piece of dough. Press dough down around filling. Cut out individual raviolis. Press down edges with a fork. Repeat with dough and filling. Cook until al dente in boiling, well-salted water. Top with Parmesan cream and garnish with fresh Parmesan, fresh mint, romaine lettuce and pea shoots.

Wine Pairing:

La Puerta — Torrontes

Aris's Wine Notes: The Torrontes grape, an Argentine specialty, has yielded a lovely and elegant wine in the hands of La Puerta. The overall impression is one of delicacy, but the wine has hidden strengths that emerge as soon as the wine is challenged by the food. The dish is quite elegant and subtle, yet is rich enough to require a palate cleansing wash by this delightful wine. Fortunately for the consumer, La Puerta's quality comes at a friendly price.

Thom's Tips: Parmesan cheese rinds may have the texture of old shoes, but they still have a great flavor. When creating an Italian white sauce, you can take the cheese rinds and steep them in the heated cream to add extra cheese flavor. Just take them out before you thicken the sauce.

Goat Cheese Gnocchi
with Vegetables, Arugula and Basil Pesto

From: Inn on Biltmore Estate • 1 Approach Road • Asheville, NC 28803

2 tablespoons butter

1 shallot, sliced thin

3 cloves garlic, sliced thin

8 baby squash, sliced

4 baby gold beets, peeled and
    blanched

1 head cauliflower, cut into small
    florets and blanched

20 asparagus tips, blanched

¼ cup English peas, blanched

12 green beans, blanched

12 baby tomatoes

Gnocchi (see recipe below)

Pesto (see recipe below)

4 black mission figs, quartered

shaved Parmesan

4 squash blossoms

olive oil

Gnocchi

8 ounces goat cheese, softened

2 egg yolks

¾ cup semolina flour

¼ cup all-purpose flour

kosher salt to taste

Pesto

½ cup basil leaves

3 cloves garlic

1 teaspoon pine nuts, toasted

In a skillet over medium heat, add butter. Sauté the shallot and 3 cloves garlic. Add the squash, beets, cauliflower and asparagus and cook for 2 minutes. Toss in the peas, green beans, tomatoes and Gnocchi and heat for 2 minutes more. Finish with the Pesto, season and transfer to a bowl and garnish with fresh figs, shaved Parmesan, squash blossoms and olive oil.

Gnocchi: Soften goat cheese in a bowl. Add egg yolks. Fold the semolina flour in by hand. Once incorporated, slowly add half the all-purpose flour. Add more flour if needed to obtain a smooth consistency. Season with salt and roll into logs about 1 inch thick. Cut 1 to 1 ½-inch portions and score with the tip of a fork. Blanch in heavy salted boiling water and set aside.

Pesto: In a blender, add the basil leaves, 3 cloves garlic, pine nuts, lemon juice and olive oil and blend for 2 minutes. Slowly add the cheese to finish. Season with salt and pepper.

Wine Pairing:

Biltmore Estate —— Sauvignon Blanc

Aris's Wine Notes: The flavors of Sauvignon Blanc have an affinity for goat cheese and also for vegetables, making it a natural choice for this dish. Biltmore does a nice job creating such a lively wine with inviting fruity aromas, ripe flavors carrying a clear varietal identity and finishing with a lemony tart edge.

2 lemons, juiced
¼ cup olive oil
¼ cup grated Parmesan cheese
salt and pepper

Makes 4 servings

Thom's Tips: When squeezing a lemon place one hand under the lemon to catch the seeds. As the juice runs through your fingers you can direct where the juice goes. It also beats trying to pick the seeds out of your food afterwards.

Pesto and Ricotta Pizza

From: Salty Caper • 115 South Lee Street • Salisbury, NC 28144

1 Pizza Dough ball (see below)
1 cup flour
½ cup Pesto Ricotta (see below)
mozzarella, grated or sliced
1 ripe tomato, sliced
3 basil leaves, chiffonnade cut
pine nuts

Pizza Dough

1½ cups water (100–110 degrees F)
1 tablespoon and 1 teaspoon yeast
¼ teaspoon sugar
1 cup high-gluten flour
1 teaspoon semolina flour
2 teaspoons salt
2 to 3½ cups all-purpose flour

Pesto Ricotta

5 bunches fresh basil leaves, packed
¼ cup pine nuts or walnuts
¾ cup olive oil
1 to 2 garlic cloves
⅔ cup grated Romano cheese
¼ cup ricotta

Makes 1 to 2 pizzas

Thom's Tips: Basil pesto keeps in the refrigerator 1 week or in a freezer for a few months. When making it for pasta, increase the cheese amount.

Preheat oven to 450 degrees F.

On a hard surface sprinkle some flour. Place dough ball on surface and spread it flat until it reaches about 12 inches. Sprinkle flour on pizza pallet or a cutting board. Put pizza crust on it. Evenly spread Pesto Ricotta mixture over crust. Add mozzarella and sliced tomatoes. Slide pizza onto a preheated pizza stone. Cook for 10 minutes at 450 degrees F. When done, slide pizza back onto a pizza pallet or cutting board. Add basil and pine nuts. Cut into slices or serve whole.

Pizza Dough: Add water, yeast and sugar to a bowl with a pinch of high-gluten flour to feed the yeast; let sit for 10 minutes. Add semolina and salt to high-gluten flour. Mix with activated water and yeast (make sure the yeast has activated). Add all-purpose flour 1 cup at a time until you get dough. Cover dough and let rise. Punch down and cut to weight. Knead into balls.

Pesto Ricotta: Place basil leaves, pine nuts, olive oil and garlic in a food processor. Whip until well chopped and blended. Remove the mixture from the food processor and put it in a mixing bowl. Using a rubber spatula, scrape the sides of the food processor clean. Fold the Romano cheese into the mixture using the rubber spatula. Take about ¼ cup of the pesto and mix with ¼ cup ricotta. Incorporate well and set aside for pizza.

Beer Pairing:
Cottonwood American Wheat Ale —— Carolina Beer Company

Aris's Beer Notes: Although I love wine, sometimes only a brew will do. The Carolina Beer Company is top notch in all their beer styles and this American Wheat is no exception. The beer had just the right amount of weight and flavor intensity for the pizza to blend in with it and refresh the palate but not overwhelm it.

Pizza Del
Salumiere

From: Salty Caper • 115 South Lee Street • Salisbury, NC 28144

1 Pizza Dough ball (see recipe
  below)

½ cup tomato sauce or pizza sauce

1 ball fresh or dry mozzarella

4 slices prosciutto ham

1 cup balsamic vinegar, reduced by
  two-thirds

1 handful fresh arugula

Pizza Dough

1½ cups water (100–110 degrees F)

1 tablespoon and 1 teaspoon yeast

¼ teaspoon sugar

1 cup high-gluten flour

1 teaspoon semolina flour

2 teaspoons salt

2 to 3½ cups all-purpose flour

Makes 2 pizzas

Thom's Tips: Most three year olds throw pizza dough better than I do. But when I punch a hole in the middle of the dough, there is an easy fix. Just pinch the dough back together and continue on. Also, when you are finished and the pizza dough is in a lopsided circle, you can always cut it into a perfect circle with your pizza cutter.

Preheat oven to 450 degrees F, with a pizza stone placed on the top shelf.

Spread dough on a floured surface. Add tomato sauce evenly over dough. Add fresh mozzarella then prosciutto slices. Cook for 10 minutes on the stone.

Pour balsamic vinegar in a saucepan and reduce on medium-high heat until syrup consistency.

Toss arugula with the balsamic reduction. Use as a topping on the pizza when it comes out of the oven.

Pizza Dough: Add water, yeast and sugar to a bowl with a pinch of high-gluten flour to feed the yeast; let sit for 10 minutes. Add semolina and salt to high-gluten flour. Mix with activated water and yeast (make sure the yeast has activated). Add all-purpose flour 1 cup at a time until you get dough. Cover dough and let rise. Punch down and cut to weight. Knead into balls.

Wine Pairing:
Sobon — Old Vine Zinfandel

Aris's Wine Notes: The low-yielding, organically grown, ancient Zinfandel vines planted in the unique Amador microclimate yield a marvelous fruit bomb Zin. I love pairing Zinfandel with Italian food. Current DNA evidence now proves that Zinfandel is cousin to the Primitivo grape of southern Italy.

Smoked Duck and Goat Cheese Pizzetta

From: Inn on Biltmore Estate • 1 Approach Road • Asheville, NC 28803

1 tablespoon sugar

2 cups all-purpose flour

½ teaspoon salt

2 tablespoons olive oil

¼ cup canola oil

2 to 3 cloves garlic, minced

1 tablespoon dry yeast

1 cup warm water

Dinner Toppings

¼ cup kalamata olives

2 tablespoons olive oil

1 package smoked duck breast

4 to 5 tomato slices

3 tablespoons goat cheese

5 to 6 basil leaves, chopped

6 to 8 arugula leaves

black pepper

Makes 4 to 5 pizzettas

Thom's Tips: Placing your dough on the backside of a pie pan allows you to conform the dough to a specific size. It also gives you something to hold on to when you place the dough on the grill. I like having a buffer between my skin and the grill flame.

In a mixing bowl using a dough hook attachment, combine the sugar, flour, salt, oils and garlic. Add the yeast and turn mixer on slow speed. Slowly add water, starting with ½ cup. Add remaining water a little at a time until fully incorporated and the dough pulls away from the side of the bowl. Continue to mix on low to medium speed for 3 to 4 minutes. Transfer to a large bowl and cover with a dry towel and proof for 8 to 10 minutes, or until doubled. Punch down dough and proof one more time until doubled again. Punch down again and portion the dough to 4 or 5 equal pieces.

Turn your grill to high (allow to preheat 10 to 15 minutes). Meanwhile, lay one portion of the dough on a flat, lightly oiled pan. (I like to use the back side of a large pie pan or baking sheet.) Press the dough down and gently form into a circle. Once the dough is formed, turn your pan upside down so the dough sits flat on the grill and then let set 1 to 2 minutes. Remove the pan. Flip the dough over and mark the other side.

Dinner Toppings: In a blender, add the kalamata olives and olive oil. Blend until you form a smooth purée. Slice the smoked duck and tomatoes into small bite-sized pieces. Spread the olive purée on the pizzetta. Add the duck and tomato. Crumble the goat cheese on top. If you desire, heat in the oven for 3 to 4 minutes. Top with fresh basil and arugula. Brush with olive oil and finish with cracked pepper.

Wine Pairing:

Biltmore Estate — Sangiovese

Aris's Wine Notes: Sangiovese is the major grape used in Chianti and is perfectly suited to this dish. The spiced cherry fruit has a nice sense of richness and molds itself to the wide range of flavors in the dish. There was just enough tannin and acidity to cut through the fat of the duck and cheese while the oaky flavors complement the smokiness in the duck.

Fish & Seafood

Pan-Seared Sea Bass
over Asparagus Crab Salad and Tangerine Soy Wasabi Sauce

From: Christopher's New Global Cuisine • 712 Brookstown Avenue • Winston-Salem, NC 27101

1 tablespoon cumin

1 cup flour

4 (7- to 8-ounce) sea bass fillets

½ cup oil, divided

1 bunch asparagus

1 large tomato

2 cups crabmeat

salt and pepper

1 cup tangerine juice

½ cup sugar

1 teaspoon wasabi powder

½ cup soy sauce

Makes 4 servings

Thom's Tips: Asparagus ends often taste like you're gnawing on a pencil. It's best to break the ends off of fresh asparagus. Where to break is determined by the asparagus itself. Just take the asparagus stalk in two hands. Hold it with one hand below the leafy tip and with your other hand at the very end of the stalk. Bend the stalk until it breaks. The stalk usually breaks right along the line of the flexible "good to eat" part and the tough woody "not fun to eat" part.

Preheat oven to 500 degrees F.

Mix cumin with flour. Flour one side of fish in seasoned flour. Heat 1/4 cup of oil in sauté pan. Sear floured side of fish for 2 minutes. Flip and transfer to oven; bake 4 to 6 minutes.

Bring water to a boil and blanch asparagus; remove asparagus and place in ice water. Chop after cooled. Dice tomato and then place asparagus and tomato in a bowl with crabmeat; mix well. While fish is in oven, heat ¼ cup oil in sauté pan. Add crab asparagus mixture and sauté for 2 minutes. Season with salt and pepper.

In a saucepan, mix tangerine juice, sugar, wasabi powder and soy sauce; bring to a boil. After it is boiling, lower heat and let reduce by one-fourth. Simmer 10 to 15 minutes.

Ladle sauce into a bowl. Spoon on crab mixture. Place fish on top.

Wine Pairing
Marqués de Cáceres — Rioja Blanco

Aris's Wine Notes: The name Rioja usually brings visions of the world famous reds. Overlooked are the lovely, versatile and affordable whites made from Spain's indigenous Viura grape. A delicate nose of pears, apples and white flowers is followed on the palate with mineral notes and a refreshing lemony acidity. The elegance and finesse of the wine matches the same qualities of the dish.

Asian
Sea Bass

From: City Tavern Hearst Tower • 215 South Tryon Suite D • Charlotte, NC 28202

Sprinkle each side of sea bass with salt and pepper. Place in a sauté pan with ginger and white wine. Cover sauté pan and poach until fish is cooked. Turn frequently.

Place oil and garlic in a hot sauté pan. Add orange juice, pineapple juice, sake, chicken stock and soy sauce. Add spinach to sauce and blanch. DO NOT COOK.

In a small pot, place 2 cups rice with 4 cups water. Simmer until all liquid has evaporated, approximately 15 to 20 minutes. Season with salt and pepper.

Place fish in pasta bowl on top of rice and top with the sauce.

Wine Pairing:

Tango Sur — Chardonnay

Aris's Wine Notes: Whenever the wine talk turns to Argentina, the word "value" is virtually always used in the same breath. Tango Sur is a fun and inexpensive wine to drink. This Chardonnay provides a nice canvas onto which a chef can showcase a superb dish like this.

4 (8-ounce) sea bass fillets
1 pinch salt and pepper
2 pinches fresh ginger
¼ cup white wine
3 tablespoons oil
1 pinch chopped garlic
1 cup orange juice
1 cup pineapple juice
½ cup sake
½ cup chicken stock
6 tablespoons soy sauce
handful fresh spinach
2 cups rice
4 cups water

Makes 4 servings

Thom's Tips: To flavor your rice when cooking it, substitute chicken or beef stock for the water. You can also add your favorite herbs in addition to salt and pepper.

Pan-Seared Sea Bass
with a Lemon, Caper, Tomato and White Wine Sauce

From: Gianni & Gaitano's • 14460-171 New Falls of the Neuse Road • Raleigh, NC 27614

4 (6-ounce) sea bass fillets

salt and pepper

flour

olive oil

1 teaspoon chopped shallots

1 tomato, chopped

¼ teaspoon capers

½ cup white wine

½ cup chicken stock

juice of ½ lemon

1 tablespoon butter

¼ teaspoon chives, chopped

Makes 4 servings

Thom's Tips: You will know when the olive oil is ready for sautéing when it "shimmers." Shimmering is when your oil is just about ready to burn. If your oil starts to smoke, it is too hot and you should start over. Shimmering olive oil will have a slightly glazed look to it and will be very, very fluid.

Preheat oven to 350 degrees F.

Season sea bass with salt and pepper and then dredge in flour. Coat a pan with olive oil and heat until hot (oil will shimmer). Sear fish on both sides (about 2 minutes per side) and then bake in oven for 5 minutes.

Remove excess oil from the pan and put back over medium heat. Add shallots, tomato and capers. Cook for another minute, or until shallots are tender. Add wine and cook for 30 seconds. Add the chicken stock, lemon juice, butter and chives. Add salt and pepper to taste.

Place sea bass on plate. Ladle sauce over fish.

Wine Pairing:
Simi — Russian River Reserve Chardonnay

Aris's Wine Notes: The grapes for this Simi Reserve deliver vivid, blossomy fruit flavors, suggestive of apples, lemons and tropical fruit. The fruit is enriched by creamy, toasty oak, which never intrudes on the basic Chardonnay. On the palate, the luscious ripeness is buoyed by generous acidity, providing refreshment and food handling capabilities.

Blackened Fish and Pineapple and Melon Salsa

From: Cajun Queen • 1800 East 7th Street • Charlotte, NC 28204

Preheat oven to 350 degrees F.

Lightly oil the fish and then coat with blackening seasoning. Blacken in a cast-iron skillet or on the grill. When fish is blackened on both sides, place on oven pan. Bake in oven until desired doneness is reached.

Oil and season scallops with blackening spices. Blacken in cast-iron skillet. Reserve until fish is cooked. Place fish and scallops on plate. Top with salsa.

Pineapple and Melon Salsa: Cut the top and bottom off the pineapple and then peel. Cut melon in half and remove seeds. Cut melon and pineapple into large chunks. Mix all ingredients together, tossing with lime juice; set aside.

Wine Pairing:
St. Christopher — Riesling

Aris's Wine Notes: Blackening spices pose a problem for many dry wines as they seem even drier and make the food seem hotter. A dry but richly fruited Chardonnay would work, but most come with oaky flavors. This dish has enough of a smoky taste from the spices and grill pan. German Rieslings offer a delightful companion for this dish with their delicate floral notes, lightly sweet fruitiness and refreshing, citrus acidity.

1 teaspoon vegetable oil
4 (8-ounce) fillets of your favorite fish
4 teaspoons blackening spice
8 diver or dry-packed scallops

Pineapple and Melon Salsa
½ pineapple
½ cantaloupe
½ jalapeño pepper
1 teaspoon diced red bell pepper
1 teaspoon diced red onion
1 teaspoon chopped cilantro
1 teaspoon fresh lime juice
pinch salt

Makes 4 servings

Thom's Tips: There are some spices that only become flavorful when exposed to hot oil, such as cumin and curry. For example, when you are blackening foods, make sure that they are cooking in a little oil, otherwise they will not be as flavorful as expected.

Seared Flounder, Kale and Cucumber Salad, Watermelon Vinaigrette and Vegetables

From: Cafe on the Square • One Biltmore Avenue • Asheville, NC 28801

4 flounder fillets

black pepper

salt

powdered onion

2 tablespoons olive oil

Warm Kale and Cucumber Salad

2 bundles fresh kale

1 large cucumber, diced

4 tablespoons butter

¼ cup shallot purée (about 2 shallots)

¼ cup white wine

salt and pepper to taste

Watermelon Vinaigrette

½ seedless watermelon

¼ cup red onion purée (about ½ red onion)

¾ cup red wine vinegar

¼ cup champagne

½ cup granular sugar

1 tablespoon chopped fresh cilantro

1 cup olive oil

Makes 4 servings

Thom's Tips: When straining food through cheesecloth, double the cloth by forming an "X" with the two sheets. This not only filters the liquid even more, but it also provides an extra layer in case you tear part of the cheesecloth.

Preheat oven to 350 degrees F.

Lightly season one side of fish with pepper, salt and powdered onion while heating the pan to medium-high. Add enough oil to barely cover pan. Place seasoned side of fish down. Cook for about 1 minute, or until golden brown. Flip and do the same to the other side. Finish baking in the oven for 5 minutes. Serve in pasta dish. Put Watermelon Vinaigrette in first, then the warm Kale and Cucumber Salad, followed by the fish on top.

Warm Kale and Cucumber Salad: De-stem kale and chop into bite-size pieces. Dice cucumber about 1/4 inch. Heat sauté pan to medium heat. Melt butter and add shallot purée. Turn heat up and add chopped kale. Add wine, splash-by-splash, and toss. Add cold cucumber with salt and pepper. (The objective is not to cook the cucumber.)

Watermelon Vinaigrette: Cut watermelon in half. Then quarter and cut into chunks. Process in food processor. Strain with cheesecloth to get juice. Add onion purée to watermelon juice. Add vinegar, champagne, sugar, cilantro and olive oil; whisk.

Wine Pairing:
Holly's Garden - Pinot Gris

Aris's Wine Notes: Australian Pinot Gris makes a unique statement, different from Italian Pinot Grigio, Oregon Pinot Gris or Alsace Pinot Gris, which is the homeland for this grape. This wine has a fatter and softer palate with flavors leaning more towards tropical fruits. Its backbone is solid without being tart.

Grouper with Horseradish Hash Browns

From: 45 South • 20 East Broad Street • Savannah, GA 31401

Preheat oven to 350 degrees F.

Place horseradish, potato, onion and thyme in water. Let stand for 5 to 10 minutes. Remove from water.

Season both sides of grouper with a pinch of salt and pepper, then flour. Lightly place horseradish crust atop fish. Dust with flour. Place in pan with olive oil over medium-high heat. Cook until golden brown. Flip fish. Deglaze pan with white wine. Finish in the oven.

Infuse cream with pickling spice, garlic and shallots. Steep for 15 minutes on medium-high heat. Whisk in roux until sauce consistency. Cook for 10 to 15 minutes to cook out flour.

Reduce cognac to syrup consistency and then fold into cream sauce. Strain sauce through fine mesh sieve. Add crumbled Stilton cheese.

Blanch green beans and carrot in boiling water. Heat butter and sauté shallots until softened. Season pan with salt and pepper. Transfer vegetables to sauté pan and lightly sauté.

Ladle sauce into plates. Place fish on sauce. Top with sautéed vegetables.

Wine Pairing:
Wente —Livermore Valley Chardonnay

Aris's Wine Notes: Wente's unique Livermore Valley soil and climate combine to give a richly textured Chardonnay with ripe tropical and crisp citrus fruit flavors. A gentle kiss of oak and yeasty notes add complexity, and a light vanilla spice sweetens up the acidity in the finish. The wine is gentle enough for the grouper yet strong enough for the blue cheese.

½ cup horseradish root, washed, peeled and grated
1 cup grated Yukon gold potato
1 Vidalia onion, peeled and grated
pinch of fresh thyme
4 (6- to 8-ounce) grouper fillets
salt and pepper
½ cup flour
2 tablespoons olive oil
¼ cup white wine
1 pint cream
1½ teaspoons pickling spice
1 clove garlic, peeled
3 shallots, sliced
⅓ cup cognac
⅛ cup crumbled Stilton cheese
1 pound green beans
1 carrot, peeled and julienned
2 tablespoons butter
pinch of diced shallot
salt and pepper to taste

Roux
½ cup flour, ½ cup water

Makes 4 servings

Thom's Tips: To avoid crying when cutting onions, put the onion in the refrigerator for an hour or two before cutting. Cooling them down should help contain the acids that are released when an onion is sliced.

Pan-Roasted Grouper with Fresh Corn, Tomatoes and Arugula

From: Frazier's Bistro • 2418 Hillsborough Street • Raleigh, NC 27607

1 tablespoon whole cumin seeds, toasted

4 grouper fillets, preferably local

salt and pepper

1 tablespoon butter, plus more for cooking

4 sprigs fresh thyme, removed from stalks and chopped

4 ears fresh corn, cleaned and de-silked

½ cup milk

salt and pepper to taste

1 tablespoon grated Parmesan cheese

¼ cup mascarpone

4 beefsteak tomatoes, as ripe as possible

¼ cup sherry vinegar

½ to ¾ cup extra virgin olive oil, plus a splash for salad

2 cups arugula

1 pint cherry or Sungold tomatoes, cut in half

1 tablespoon chopped shallots

extra virgin olive oil

salt and pepper to taste

Makes 4 servings

Preheat oven to 400 degrees F.

Grind the cumin seeds into a fine powder. Lightly sprinkle on the fish. Set aside in the refrigerator for 20 to 40 minutes.

Remove the fish from the fridge and season with salt and pepper. Heat some oil in a pan over high heat, and sear the fish skin side down for about 2 minutes. Slide the pan in the oven and finish cooking, another 5 to 7 minutes, depending on thickness. Carefully remove from the oven and add a small amount of butter and thyme to the tops of the fillets to finish.

Cut the kernels off the corn cobs, reserving ½ cup. Using a box grater, shred the cleaned cobs, removing extra kernels and corn juice. Place the corn and milk into a blender and blend until smooth. Strain into a medium pot and cook over low heat until a thick consistency is reached. It should look like polenta. Meanwhile, sauté the reserved kernels in butter and season with salt and pepper. Fold them into the polenta with the butter and cheeses. Keep the polenta warm until ready to serve.

Bring a large pot of water to a boil. Prepare an ice bath in a large bowl. Core and score the tomatoes. Blanch them quickly in the boiling water (about 15 seconds). Remove from boiling water and shock in the ice bath. Peel the tomatoes and squeeze out the seeds. Put the tomatoes in a blender with the vinegar and begin to purée. Drizzle in the olive oil, tasting until you have a balanced vinaigrette; set aside.

Sauté the arugula and tomatoes together in a skillet with the shallots and some extra virgin olive oil, salt and pepper.

Ladle the tomato vinaigrette on a plate. Spoon on the polenta. Add the sautéed vegetables and then top with the grouper.

<u>Wine Pairing:</u>
Blackstone — Pinot Grigio

Aris's Wine Notes: Blackstone Pinot Grigio delivers a lovely floral aroma laced with citrus and a refreshingly crisp and light-bodied texture. Paired with this dish, the enjoyment of both the wine and food are enhanced. The dish benefited from the wine's mouth-cleansing qualities while the wine gained some of the complex flavors of the dish without being overwhelmed by them.

Thom's Tips: To roughly grind spices, such as toasted cumin seeds, use a spice grinder. If you're like me and don't have a spice grinder, a coffee grinder is a perfect substitute. Just remember to clean out your coffee grinder when you're finished, or tomorrow's coffee will taste a little weird. Ummmmm toasted cumin seed coffee . . .

Tammy Dyer's
Almond Grouper

From: Red Rocks Café • 4223-8 Providence Road • Charlotte, NC 28211

1 cup sliced almonds

1 cup breadcrumbs, panko preferred

1 teaspoon salt and pepper

4 (8-ounce) grouper fillets

1 tablespoon canola oil

¼ cup Gran Marnier

1 cup orange juice

¼ pound butter, unsalted

¼ cup sugar

1 cup balsamic vinegar

4 cups cooked rice

1½ cups heavy cream

4 tablespoons unsalted butter

4 tablespoons grated Romano cheese

12 stalks asparagus

extra virgin olive oil

1 clove garlic, minced

salt and pepper to taste

¼ cup alfalfa sprouts

Make 4 servings

Thom's Tips: Not sure what to do with plain leftover rice? Create instant risotto. Heat rice with cream. Add a splash of white wine for flavor. Finish off with butter and cheese. Quick and easy.

Purée almonds till fine. Add breadcrumbs and purée to a powder. Add salt and pepper. Dredge grouper in almond crust. Sear in hot sauté pan with oil until brown on both sides and cooked through.

Combine Gran Marnier and orange juice in a saucepan. Reduce to a syrup. Whip butter slowly into Gran Marnier reduction and then add sugar.

Reduce balsamic vinegar in a saucepan until syrupy.

Sauté cooked rice with cream. Add butter and cheese; cook and stir until creamy.

Blanch asparagus in boiling water. Sauté blanched asparagus in oil, garlic, salt and pepper.

Ladle sauce onto plate. Add rice. Place asparagus and fish on rice. Drizzle plate with balsamic reduction. Garnish with alfalfa sprouts.

<u>Wine Pairing:</u>
Monkey Bay — Sauvignon Blanc

Aris's Wine Notes: We needed a fairly substantial wine for this dish, considering the cream and reduction sauces have added richness of texture and concentration of flavors. Sauvignon Blanc grapes grown in the Marlborough region of New Zealand have the right stuff. The cool climate, long sunny days and long growing season yield wines of firm acid structure and great physiological ripeness.

La Cava Grouper
alla Putanesca

From: La Cava Restaurant • **329 South Church Street** • **Salisbury, NC 28144**

Preheat oven to 450 degrees F.

Salt and pepper fish. Place fish skin side down in a heated non-stick sauté pan with 1 tablespoon olive oil; sear the skin. Flip and place in the oven. Bake for 6 to 9 minutes.

In a sauté pan, heat remaining olive oil, garlic and anchovies. Make sure that the anchovies dissolve into the oil. When the garlic is golden, add the tomatoes, olives, capers and tomato sauce; reduce. Once you have the consistency that you need, remove from heat and add basil.

Heat vegetable oil in a sauté pan. Fry your bread on both sides for about 3 minutes; remove and pat dry with a paper towel. Place the fried bread in a bowl or plate.

Ladle sauce on top of the bread. Place your fish gently on top of both. Drizzle some olive oil on the plate and the fish. Finish with more basil chiffonnade.

Wine Pairing:

Albert Mann — Pinot Auxerrois

Aris's Wine Notes: Pinot Auxerrois is a unique grape from Alsace, one of the world's greatest white wine regions. The richness and natural spiciness of Alsatian wines is especially friendly to Mediterranean-style dishes like this, which express the fresh taste of the ingredients.

salt and pepper
4 (8-ounce) grouper fillets
3 tablespoons olive oil, divided
3 cloves garlic, chopped
1 to 2 anchovies, finely chopped
2 cups large diced tomatoes
1 cup olives
2 tablespoons capers
splash of tomato sauce (optional)
basil leaves, chiffonnade
1 cup vegetable oil
4 thick slices hard-crust bread

Makes 4 servings

Thom's Tips: If you have tomatoes that are not quite as juicy and sweet as you like, roast them. Cut them in half. Place them on a roasting pan. Season with salt and pepper and fresh herbs. Bake at 400 degrees F for 15 minutes. Remove from oven. Once they have cooled, peel off the skins. Serve as a side, as a garnish, and in salads.

Roasted Halibut
with Radicchio
and Creamed Corn

From: Four Square Restaurant • **2701 Chapel Hill Road** • **Durham, NC 27707**

2 cups heavy cream

2 ears corn, in husk

1 tablespoon fresh chopped thyme

2 tablespoons butter

2 shallots, thinly sliced

3 cloves garlic, minced

2 jalapeño peppers, seeds removed
   and minced

¼ cup minced red bell pepper

½ cup white wine

salt and pepper to taste

2 lemons

1 head radicchio

2 tablespoons finely chopped parsley

1 tablespoon extra virgin olive oil

1 tablespoon balsamic vinegar

1 tablespoon cooking oil

4 (5-ounce) halibut fillets

¼ cup thinly sliced green onion

Makes 4 servings

Preheat oven to 350 degrees F.

Put cream in a saucepot over medium heat. Cut corn kernels from the cob. Scrape the corn milk from the cob. Cut cobs into 1-inch sections; add to the pot with the cream and chopped thyme. Simmer over low to medium heat for 10 minutes.

Melt butter in a sauté pan over medium heat. Add shallots, garlic, jalapeños, corn and corn milk to the pan and then sweat for 2 minutes; do not brown. Add the bell pepper and continue to sweat for 1 minute. Add the wine and reduce over medium to high heat by two-thirds.

Strain the corncobs from the cream and then add the cream to the corn mixture; reduce over medium to high heat to a sauce-like consistency. Season with salt and pepper to taste and the juice of 1 lemon.

Cut the radicchio into quarters, cut out the core and slice lengthwise into fine strands. Place in a mixing bowl and toss with parsley, extra virgin olive oil and balsamic vinegar. Season with salt and pepper and the juice of the remaining lemon.

Heat cooking oil in a pan until very hot. Season the halibut with salt and pepper. Add the halibut to the pan and cook until it develops a brown crust (approximately 1 minute on each side). Finish cooking in oven for approximately 4 minutes.

Ladle creamed corn onto plate. Add radicchio. Top with halibut. Garnish with sliced green onion.

Wine Pairing:

King Estate — Pinot Gris

Aris's Wine Notes: Apples, citrus and melon are but a few of the flavors that come to mind when smelling and tasting this "fruit basket" of a wine. This wine also serves double duty as an anytime sipping wine as well as a food wine. The dish and wine are solid and rich but not heavy. The halibut has not been spiced or sauced to detract from its natural flavors.

Thom's Tips: Kosher salt is a favorite of chefs because of how easy it is to use. The larger grains make it easier to handle when seasoning the dish. The flatness of the grains enables you to taste the salt more by providing more surface area to the tongue, therefore requiring less salt in the dish.

Mahi-Mahi
en Cartoccio

From: Mia Famiglia • 19918 North Cove Road • Cornelius, NC 28031

½ pound unsalted butter, softened

¼ cup capers

8 anchovy fillets

salt and pepper

4 pieces parchment paper

4 (8-ounce) mahi-mahi fillets

2 tablespoons olive oil

2 tablespoons minced garlic

2 pounds baby spinach, minced

2 cups chicken stock

1 cup milk

1½ cups coarse polenta

½ cup mascarpone cheese

½ cup grated Parmesan or Romano

Tomato Relish

1 pint grape tomatoes

1 teaspoon shredded basil

1 teaspoon shredded mint

salt and pepper

¼ cup balsamic vinegar

Makes 4 servings

Thom's Tips: Anchovies—the little fish with big flavor. I ate an anchovy on the set. It felt like I had just swallowed a good portion of the Atlantic Ocean. It was then I learned anchovies are a wonderful condiment in moderation. Grind 'em, purée 'em, cut 'em so thin they melt when sautéed. It's a wonderful flavor, just cut back on the salt that you use in the rest of the recipe.

Preheat oven to 400 degrees F.

In a food processor, add softened butter, capers, anchovies, salt and pepper. Blend thoroughly. Lay out parchment paper and place about ½ tablespoon butter mixture in the center of each piece. Place filet on top. Salt and pepper each filet. Spread another ½ tablespoon butter mixture on top of each filet. Pick up the two sides of the paper, meeting in the middle, and fold down three times. Then crimp the ends of the paper. Place in oven for 15 minutes, depending on the thickness of the fillet.

Heat 2 tablespoons olive oil on medium-high heat and add garlic. As the garlic begins to get lightly toasted, add the baby spinach and continue to stir with tongs. Cook time approximately 90 seconds.

Bring chicken stock and milk to a simmer and add polenta. Simmer on low heat, continually stirring, until polenta is tender; whip in cheeses until mixed. Salt and pepper to taste. Serve fish in the paper. Simply open the paper and roll back the sides. Spoon on spinach and Tomato Relish.

Tomato Relish: Heat a small amount of oil in a sauté pan on high heat. Add tomatoes, basil, mint, salt and pepper. Sauté for about 1 minute, then add balsamic vinegar and cook for 1 more minute. Tomatoes should remain semi-firm. Serve warm.

Wine Pairing:
House of Nobilo — Sauvignon Blanc

Aris's Wine Notes: While mahi-mahi is a rather delicate fish, in this recipe it is surrounded by strong flavors and rich textures. What better for pairing than Nobilo's Sauvignon Blanc from Marlborough, New Zealand. Each mouthful has a different combination of flavors and the wine responds with aplomb, creating another flavor experience.

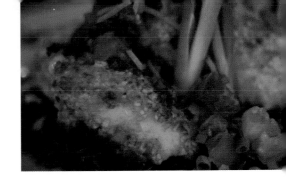

Cashew-Crusted Red Snapper with Coconut Rum Sauce

From: Key West Grill • 1214 Celebrity Circle # R7 • Myrtle Beach, SC 29577

Preheat oven to 350 degrees F.

Wash fillets and dip each in egg wash. Roll in crushed cashews until encrusted. Sauté in olive oil and butter until golden brown on each side. Add salt and pepper to taste. Add wine and lemon juice. Finish in oven, being careful not to overcook.

Garnish with Coconut Rum Sauce, carrots and tomatoes, and serve warm.

Coconut Rum Sauce: Mix coconut cream, rum and wine in small saucepan. Bring to a boil. Remove from heat.

Wine Pairing:
Liberty School — Chardonnay

Aris's Wine Notes: The vineyards of the Santa Lucia Highlands are cooled by breezes from Monterey Bay, allowing the grapes to mature at a long, slow and even pace. This keeps the acidity bright and the fruit fresh, but not at the expense of the sun-ripened richness we've come to expect from California Chardonnay. This Liberty School Chardonnay is a flexible, food-friendly wine and this is a very wine-friendly dish, a great win-win situation.

4 (8-ounce) red snapper fillets
1 cup egg wash (two eggs and
   1 cup milk)
1½ cups crushed cashews
⅓ cup olive oil
2 tablespoons butter
salt and pepper
¼ cup white wine
juice of 1 lemon
carrots, grated
tomatoes, diced

Coconut Rum Sauce

1 cup coconut cream, such as
   Coco Lopez
2 tablespoons coconut rum
2 tablespoons white wine

Makes 4 servings

Thom's Tips: A recurring theme of many chefs on *Carolina Cooking* has been to place fish into an extremely hot sauté pan, searing in the fillet's juices, keeping the fish moist and tender. Olive oil has a low burning temperature, but when olive oil is mixed with butter you can get the pan much hotter to better sear the fish.

Orange Roughy Fillet Napoletana with Portobello Mushrooms

From: Villa Romana • **707 South Kings Hwy** • **Myrtle Beach, SC 29577**

8 Roma tomatoes, sliced ⅛ inch thick

extra virgin olive oil

6 to 8 fresh basil leaves, chopped

1 tablespoon chopped flat-leaf parsley

1 to 2 clove garlic, minced

4 Portobello mushrooms, 4 inches in size

salt

oil

¼ red onion, julienned

pinch of oregano

4 orange roughy fillets

salt and pepper

1 ovolone fresh mozzarella, cut in 6 to 8 slices

Spaghetti with Quick Tomato Sauce

5 Roma tomatoes

2 tablespoons extra virgin olive oil

¼ red onion, diced

salt and crushed red pepper

4 to 5 basil leaves

¼ pound spaghetti

1 tablespoon grated fresh Parmesan cheese

Makes 4 servings

Preheat oven to 500 degrees F.

Mix Roma tomatoes, oil, basil, parsley and garlic. Put several slits on each side of the mushrooms. Season with salt and oil. Put in a baking dish underside-up. Put half of tomato mixture on mushrooms. Add the onions.

Mix oregano with the remaining tomato mixture.

Season both sides of orange roughy with salt and pepper. Place on a baking dish with the remaining tomato mixture divided equally between both sides.

Cook mushrooms and orange roughy in oven and when almost done, place mozzarella slices on each of the dishes.

Place orange roughy and mushrooms on a plate. Add side of spaghetti sprinkled with Parmesan cheese.

Spaghetti with Quick Tomato Sauce: Put tomatoes (make a cross on the underside) in boiling water for 3 minutes. Remove from water and ice down. Peel them and pass through a food mill. Put oil in a small pot and sauté onion until translucent. Add tomatoes, salt, red pepper and basil.

Cook the spaghetti according to package instructions in a pot with salted water.

When done, strain, add sauce.

Wine Pairing:

Two Hands 'Lucky Country' — GSM

Aris's Wine Notes: Pairing fish with red wine is not tough. I'll usually grab a Pinot Noir or a Chianti. For this dish I wanted something a little richer to deal with the tomatoes on the fish and on the spaghetti. The Two Hands Winery makes some of my favorite Shiraz so I was confident I'd get a bold and exciting yet balanced wine. The texture is plush but not heavy and the finish long.

Thom's Tips: Portobello mushrooms are thick and meat-like. Because they soak up oils and spices, they can be placed in marinades and then cooked like steak on the stovetop, in the oven or on a grill.

Pan-Seared American Red Snapper over Cajun Sweet Potato Hash

From: Crescent Grill • 1035 Broad Street • Camden, SC 29020

oil

4 (8-ounce) red snapper fillets

salt and white pepper to taste

1 cup butter

2 links andouille sausage, diced

1 yellow bell pepper, diced

½ red onion, diced

3 cloves garlic, diced

3 stalks celery, diced

3 ears corn, cut from cob

cayenne to taste

1 tablespoon Worcestershire sauce

¼ cup bourbon

2 large sweet potatoes, diced

1 cup crawfish tails

2 cups chicken stock

2 tablespoons butter

1 lemon wedge

Makes 4 servings

Thom's Tips: When dealing with a hot pan of oil, place the fish into the pan by angling it away from you. This way when or if the oil splatters you won't need a skin graft or burn cream.

Preheat oven to 500 degrees F.

Place sauté pan over high heat and add oil. Score snapper fillets on the skin side. Season with salt and white pepper. When oil begins to smoke, place skin side up in sauté pan. Cook the snapper until golden brown. Turn over, making sure flesh is facing up and place in oven for about 5 minutes, or until done.

In a large pot, melt butter. Add diced sausage. Sauté for 2 to 3 minutes and then add pepper, onion, garlic, celery and corn. Sauté for another 5 minutes. Season with salt, pepper, cayenne and Worcestershire. Deglaze the pan with bourbon. You may get fire when the alcohol meets the hot pan. After the flame has gone down, add sweet potato and crawfish tails. Stir, mixing all ingredients together. Add chicken stock and cook until sweet potatoes are soft. Add butter at the end to give the hash a nice glossy color.

Ladle sweet potato hash onto plate. Top with snapper. Garnish with lemon wedge.

Wine Pairing:
Funky Llama - Chardonnay

Aris's Wine Notes: The Llama is the symbol of the Andes, where the grapes for this "fun" Chardonnay come from. Ripe fruit flavors of pear and apple are the product of the high elevation sunshine. No oak is used here, leaving the natural taste of the grapes to shine through and blend with the snapper and sweet potatoes. The wine's palate is fleshy and juicy, helping offset the Cajun spiciness.

Honey Lavender-Glazed Salmon with Dijon Peppercorn Sauce

From: Christopher's New Global Cuisine • 712 Brookstown Avenue • Winston-Salem, NC 27101

Preheat oven to 500 degrees F.

Season salmon with salt and pepper. Heat 2 tablespoons oil in a sauté pan and place salmon meat side down to sear. Sear for 2 minutes and flip. Transfer to oven and cook for 7 to 10 minutes. Mix honey and lavender together. Ladle honey-lavender mixture over salmon and let rest for a couple of minutes.

In a small saucepan, heat remaining oil. Add shallots and sauté. Add flour and make a roux by whisking. Add wine and mix. Add heavy cream and mix thoroughly. Reduce heat to simmer, add mustard, salt and pepper and let simmer for 5 minutes while occasionally stirring.

In same sauté pan as salmon, add green beans and sauté with salt and pepper and sliced garlic.

Ladle sauce over plate. Place salmon over sauce and garnish with French green beans.

Wine Pairing:
Heron — Chardonnay

Aris's Wine Notes: Lately, Heron makes wines in France, Spain and California. Her international flair has created wines of balance, complexity and food compatibility. Heron Chardonnay with this dish is a winning combination. Both the wine and dish possess a stylistic combination of richness and elegance and the flavors are complementary.

4 (8-ounce) fillets salmon
salt and pepper
4 tablespoons oil, divided
1 cup honey
2 tablespoons dried lavender
1 tablespoon minced shallots
2 tablespoons flour
½ cup white wine
1 cup heavy cream
¼ cup whole-grain mustard
1 cup French green beans,
    blanched
1 clove garlic, sliced
salt and pepper to taste

Makes 4 servings

Thom's Tips: When sautéing with olive oil, try not to use extra virgin olive oil to oil your pan. The extra virgin olive oil costs more and is made from the light first press of the olives. It has a lower burning temperature than regular olive oil. This means your pan cannot get as hot before adding food to sauté.

Chilled Poached Trout
with Dill Mayonnaise
and New Potato Salad

From: Grape Escape • 62 North Lexington • Asheville, NC 28801

½ cup water

½ cup white wine

salt and white pepper

4 fresh trout fillets

4 lemon slices

1 bay leaf

5 to 6 new potatoes

1 large cucumber

1 cup plain yogurt

chives, chopped

lemon juice

romaine leaf

whole dill

Dill Mayonnaise

1 teaspoon Dijon mustard

1 egg yolk

salt and pepper

⅓ cup olive oil

1 teaspoon lemon juice

1 tablespoon chopped fresh dill

Makes 4 servings

Preheat oven to 400 degrees F.

Pour water and wine in a Pyrex dish. Salt and pepper trout. Cut fillet in 1-inch pieces. Place trout fillets cut side down in Pyrex dish. Add lemon slices and bay leaf. Poach in oven for 12 minutes. With spatula, remove the fillets and place on a plate lined with a paper towel, turning the pieces with the skin facing up. With your finger on the tip of a small knife in one corner, peel skin back slowly, so as not to break your pieces. Cover with plastic wrap and refrigerate until ready to use.

Steam potatoes until cooked all the way but still remaining firm. Transfer to ice water to quickly cool.

Peel, cut in half and seed cucumber. Slice cucumber in thin slices. Toss with salt and then set aside. Before mixing in the salad, drain cucumbers.

Mix together yogurt, chopped chives, salt, pepper and lemon juice. Slice chilled potato. In a bowl mix together yogurt dressing, potatoes and drained cucumber.

Place the whole romaine leaf on one side of the plate. Spoon salad on one side of the leaf. Place trout fillets on the other half of the leaf. Place a few dabs of Dill Mayonnaise on the trout fillets or to the side. Garnish with whole dill sprigs.

Dill Mayonnaise: In a mixing bowl whisk together mustard, egg yolk, and salt and pepper. Slowly whisk in olive oil to a smooth and firm texture. Whisk in lemon juice and chopped dill. Cover with plastic wrap and reserve until serving.

Wine Pairing:
Hugues Beaulieu - Picpoul de Pinet

Aris's Wine Notes: Picpoul de Pinet is an ancient Languedoc grape that is making a revival, and with good reason. Picpoul, which means "lip-stinger" is notable for its crisp, lemony acidity, which blends with its ripe, peach-like fruit to offer a delightfully refreshing and food-friendly wine. To really enjoy wine you need to be willing to experiment.

Thom's Tips: All the ingredients can be prepared in advance, but do not assemble until ready to serve. By leaving the trout fillet whole, you can serve this recipe as a lunch entrée. Simply place the trout on top of steamed sliced new potatoes and garnish with a small salad.

Parchment Pouch
Salmon

From: 700 Drayton—Mansion on Forsyth Park • 700 Drayton Street • Savannah, GA 31401

4 (3-ounce) salmon fillets

salt and pepper

1 piece parchment paper

¾ cup thinly sliced or shaved fennel

1 orange, thinly sliced with skin on

1½ ounces candied ginger, finely
  chopped

¼ cup butter

½ cup dry white wine

Makes 4 servings

Thom's Tips: As tempting as it looks, please don't eat the parchment paper. I realize that the juices and seasonings have soaked into the paper, making it look edible. But remember it is still only paper, not food.

Preheat oven to 400 degrees F.

Season salmon with salt and pepper. Set aside.

Lay the parchment paper on the prep table and spray with non-stick spray. Place shaved fennel in center of paper. Add 3 to 4 thin slices of oranges on the fennel. Lay salmon on the oranges. Press ginger on top of salmon. Place a pad of butter on salmon and then pour the wine over the salmon. Fold in the ends of the paper to form a pouch, twist the top end of the paper and trim the excess with scissors. Place the pouch in a baking dish and bake for about 15 to 20 minutes, or until desired doneness is achieved.

To open the pouch, fold down the edges and serve in the pouch with grilled asparagus or desired vegetables.

Wine Pairing:
Muga — Rioja Rosado

Aris's Wine Notes: Muga is one of Spain's best wineries and world renowned for sensational red Rioja wines. This rosé is a lovely, refreshing sipping wine, yet has all the prerequisites to complement this elegant dish—crisp and dry on the palate but not competing with its lively, fruity personality. This is a lovely match for the salmon, which is simply cooked with only the fennel, ginger and orange for complementary flavors.

Prosciutto-Wrapped Wild Salmon with Mushroom Risotto and Garden Peas

From: Inn on Biltmore Estate • 1 Approach Road • Asheville, NC 28803

5 tablespoons butter

½ white onion, finely diced

1 cup Arborio rice

½ cup Chardonnay

4 cups hot chicken broth

salt and white pepper

8 slices prosciutto

4 (7-ounce) wild salmon fillets

olive oil

¾ cup English peas

½ teaspoon chopped garlic

1 teaspoon minced shallot

12 fresh shiitake mushrooms

8 chanterelles, morels or other
   fresh mushrooms

12 baby tomatoes

Makes 4 servings

Thom's Tips: Run your middle and forefingers across the top of the salmon fillet to feel for hidden bones.

Preheat oven to 400 degrees F.

Heat a heavy saucepan over medium heat. Add 1 tablespoon butter, then the onion and sweat. Next add rice. Stir rice around in the butter and onions. Deglaze with Chardonnay and stir using a wooden spoon or spatula. Add enough hot broth to cover the rice. Continue to stir constantly over low to medium heat. Add broth two more times while continuing to stir. Season with salt and white pepper.

While the risotto is cooking, lay 2 slices of prosciutto flat, then wrap around each piece of salmon. In a hot skillet, add a touch of olive oil. Sear the fish on all sides. Transfer the fish to the oven and continue to cook for about 5 minutes more, or until the fish is cooked through.

In a blender, add English peas with garlic, shallot and ¾ cup chicken broth; purée. Season with salt and pepper. Strain through a wire mesh strainer.

In a small hot skillet, add a teaspoon of olive oil. Add the mushrooms and sauté. Fold the mushrooms into the risotto and finish the risotto with 3 to 4 tablespoons cold butter.

Sauté the puréed English peas and baby tomatoes. Ladle peas and tomatoes on plate. Top with mushroom risotto. Place salmon on risotto.

Wine Pairing:
Biltmore Estate —— Chateau Reserve Chardonnay

Aris's Wine Notes: Biltmore's Estate Chardonnay is one of their finest wines, combining richness and structure with finesse and balance. When paired with the salmon, both were enlivened. The richness of the salmon is complemented by the ripe fruit and butterscotch flavors, while being balanced by the crisp acidity.

Cedar-Planked Salmon with Mushroom Ragout, Goat Cheese Crumbles and Pinot Reduction

From: Solstice Kitchen and Wine Bar • 841-4 Sparkleberry Lane • Columbia, SC 29229

Preheat oven to 375 degrees F.

Season salmon on both sides with salt and pepper. Sear salmon on both sides in pan with olive oil. Remove salmon from pan and place on cedar plank. (Remember to soak the plank in water.) Put in oven and bake for 7 to 10 minutes.

Pour wine in a saucepan and reduce over medium-high heat until syrup consistency.

Wild Mushroom Ragout: Sweat onion and garlic in large sauté pan with olive oil. Add the fresh mushrooms. After they are reduced, remove the mushrooms and dice them on a cutting board. Return the diced mushrooms to the pan. Add the rehydrated mushrooms and their water. Cook down until most of the water has evaporated. Add thyme and heavy cream and stir. Allow to thicken and then remove from heat.

Ladle sauce onto plate. Top with salmon. Serve with your favorite seasonal vegetables and goat cheese crumbles.

Wine Pairing:

Witness Tree — Pinot Noir

Aris's Wine Notes: Witness Tree's estate grown Pinot Noir has a classic bright garnet color with a nose full of black fruits, chocolate and a hint of spice. The wine has great structure and a very long finish. The wine and food create a lovely symphony. Pinots this rich are often too much for salmon, but the cedar, mushrooms and wine reduction made the richness of the wine a necessity.

4 (6-ounce) wild salmon fillets, skin off
salt and pepper
olive oil for sautéing
1 or 2 cedar planks (depending on size), thoroughly soaked in water
1 cup Pinot Noir
½ cup goat cheese crumbles

Wild Mushroom Ragout

1 onion, finely diced
1 clove garlic, minced
olive oil for sautéing
3 cups fresh wild mushrooms (cremini, shiitake, oyster, portobello)
1 cup dried wild mushrooms, rehydrated in 2 cups hot water
1 teaspoon thyme
¾ cup heavy cream

Makes 4 servings

Thom's Tips: When you go to a high-end grocery store, you'll see cedar planks to cook salmon on. Instead of paying the exorbitant costs for 1 plank, you can go to a home improvement store and buy untreated planks for a fraction of the cost. They work great and smell wonderful. Just remember to soak the plank before you put it in the oven or on the grill or you'll have cedar-smoked salmon.

Sweet Chile Marinated Ahi Tuna
with Black Bean Butter Sauce and Jicama Mango Slaw

From: Christopher's New Global Cuisine • 712 Brookstown Avenue • Winston-Salem, NC 271010

2 cups sweet chile sauce

1 lime

2 teaspoons chopped fresh cilantro

½ cup soy sauce

dash hot sauce

4 (8-ounce) tuna fillets

Black Bean Butter Sauce

1 (16-ounce) can black beans, undrained

1 teaspoon chile powder

1 teaspoon cumin

1 teaspoon granulated garlic

1 teaspoon onion powder

1 teaspoon salt

1 dash cayenne pepper

1 stick butter

Jicama Mango Slaw

1 cup julienned mango

1 cup julienned jicama

1 teaspoon chopped fresh cilantro

1 tablespoon oil

1 tablespoon rice wine vinegar

salt and pepper

Makes 4 servings

In a mixing bowl, combine sweet chile sauce, lime juice, cilantro, soy sauce and hot sauce; add tuna and rub until completely covered.

Sear tuna in a frying pan, 30 seconds per side. Repeat on all six sides. Remove tuna and slice into thin strips.

On a plate, ladle Black Bean Butter Sauce and then place Jicama Mango Slaw in middle of sauce. Fan tuna out over slaw. Garnish with fresh cilantro, if desired.

Black Bean Butter Sauce: In a blender, mix black beans, chile powder, cumin, granulated garlic, onion powder, salt and cayenne. Blend until smooth, then transfer to a small saucepan. Heat sauce until it starts to bubble. Cut butter into 4 pieces. While stirring with a whisk, add 1 piece of butter at a time, letting each melt before adding the next piece. Make sure to continuously stir so butter does not separate. Lower heat to low and let simmer, stirring occasionally while you prepare the slaw.

Jicama Mango Slaw: Put mango and jicama into a mixing bowl. Add cilantro, oil, vinegar, salt and pepper and mix together.

Wine Pairing:
Banrock Station — Chardonnay

Aris's Wine Notes: Banrock Station offers good quality at a price that makes them "everyday" wines. Offering the wine in a "bag-in-a-box" format gets the price even lower and keeps the wine fresh for months. A clean and crisp finish balances this easy drinking style of wine. The Chardonnay's richness was enough to balance the tuna and spices and offered fruit flavors more complementary to the jicama and mango than a red wine would.

Thom's Tips: Mangos are odd fruits. They're hard to peel. I've shot a number of mangos across the room while trying to peel them. To easily peel a mango, make an "X" across the top of the fruit where the stem comes out. Then, with your thumb and forefinger, grab part of the "X" and peel the peel down to the bottom of the fruit. Repeat this until the mango is peeled and your hands are nice and sticky.

Rice Paper–Wrapped Tuna, Salad of Mizuna and Avocado with Grapefruit-Wasabi Vinaigrette

From: Four Square Restaurant • 2701 Chapel Hill Road • Durham, NC 27707

8 rice paper wrappers

1 egg, beaten

4 (5-ounce) tuna fillets

salt and pepper

cooking oil

1½ teaspoons dry wasabi powder

1½ teaspoons water

2 shallots, minced

1 tablespoon minced ginger

1 clove minced garlic

8 small scallions, minced

2 whole ruby red grapefruits

¼ cup sherry vinegar

2 lemons, juiced

½ cup walnut oil

2 cups mizuna

1 avocado, sliced

4 radishes, shaved

Makes 4 servings

On a cutting board, lay out one rice paper wrapper to form a diamond shape. Using a pastry brush, liberally coat with egg wash. Lay a second sheet down slightly staggered to the right.

Season the tuna with salt and pepper and roll up in the wrapper, folding in the edges as you go. Brush the last flap with egg wash to seal it closed.

Heat oil in an 8-inch skillet over high heat until it just starts to smoke. Reduce the heat to medium-high and place the tuna in the pan. Cook 2 minutes per side, or until golden brown. Remove from the pan and wrap in a clean dishtowel for 1 minute to finish cooking.

In a mixing bowl, whisk together the wasabi and water until it forms a paste. Add the shallots, ginger, garlic and scallions. Add the supremes from 2 grapefruit (the grapefruit sections with the skin, rind and seeds removed) and squeeze out all the juice into the bowl. Add the vinegar and lemon juice and whisk together. Whisk in walnut oil. Season to taste with salt and pepper.

Place the mizuna, avocado and shaved radishes in a mixing bowl and season with salt and pepper.

Toss with 4 cups of the vinaigrette.

Put a fourth of the salad mix on each plate. Cut the tuna on the bias with a sharp knife. Place tuna fillet on top of the greens and ladle 1 to 1½ cups of vinaigrette over top.

Wine Pairing:

Franz Karl Schmitt — Niersteiner Olberg Riesling Kabinett

Aris's Wine Notes: Like all fine Rieslings, there is a sense of delicacy, yet the wine has the underlying strengths capable of dealing with a dish like this, full of contrasts. The juicy Riesling fruit complemented the succulence of the tuna. The heat of the wasabi and bitterness of the vegetables was handled by the wine's sweetness, while its acidity balanced the acidity in the dish.

Thom's Tips: If you are using a fresh piece of tuna, it should never smell like tuna fish from the can. It should have almost no smell. If it does have a smell, it should be of fresh sea water.

Tuna and Smoked Bacon Egg Roll with Soba Noodles and Red Curry Coconut Sauce

From: Divine Dining Group • 3993 Hwy 17 • Murrells Inlet, SC 29576

1½ pounds fresh tuna, bright red

1 pound applewood smoked bacon

8 large egg roll wrappers

1 goat cheese log

2 eggs, beaten

cornstarch

2 cups peanut or vegetable oil

1 pound soba noodles

3 tablespoons sesame oil, divided

1 tablespoon peanut or vegetable oil

1 can red curry paste

1 (13.5-ounce) can coconut milk

1 lemon, juiced

1 pound baby spinach

1 fresh mango, diced

Makes 4 servings

Thom's Tips: The mysterious mango. Mangos are best when they are perfectly ripe. But when are they perfectly ripe? Their skin has reached a greenish yellow, slightly red hue. They are slightly soft to the touch but not squishy. To make a mango ripen faster, leave it out in the room or in the sun. To slow down the ripening mango, put it in the refrigerator.

Cut tuna into eight equal rectangular pieces. Heat a sauté pan. Sear tuna on two sides. Remove from pan and cool. Cook bacon in pan until crisp; remove and drain.

To make egg rolls, lay out wrappers. Place about 2 table-spoons goat cheese in the center. Lay 1 piece of bacon and 1 piece of tuna over cheese. Roll and seal with egg wash. Roll in cornstarch and set aside. In a large saucepan, heat 2 cups oil to 350 degrees F. Fry egg rolls to a golden brown. Remove and drain well.

Boil soba noodles until cooked but still firm to the bite. Drain and rinse under cold water. Sauté soba noodles in 2 tablespoons sesame oil.

Heat 1 tablespoon oil in a medium saucepan. Add red curry paste and sauté for 45 seconds. Add coconut milk and simmer for 20 minutes. Squeeze in lemon juice. Taste, season, and set aside, keeping warm.

Sauté spinach briefly in remaining sesame oil.

To plate, twirl soba noodles in center of plate. Place spinach on top of noodles. Cut egg rolls on bias, arrange around noodles, two egg rolls per plate. Drizzle curry sauce over and around. Garnish with fresh mango.

Wine Pairing:
Estancia — Pinnacles Ranches Pinot Noir

Aris's Wine Notes: Although I can think of many white wines that would be marvelous with this tuna dish, I enjoy challenging a red wine's versatility. My champion for versatility is Pinot Noir. This Estancia illustrates with rich, supple black cherry fruit that it is delectable and easy to drink. The velvety texture veils a sturdy backbone that holds its ground against the wide range of flavors and textures delivered by this dish.

Elliot Sadler's
Sesame Tuna

From: Red Rocks Café • 4223-8 Providence Road • Charlotte, NC 28211

Dredge tuna in sesame seeds and sear in a hot pan with vegetable oil. Cook tuna till medium-rare.

Combine pineapple juice, soy sauce, vinegar, sesame oil, brown sugar, chives, sesame seeds, salt, pepper and ginger in a saucepan. Bring to a boil.

Blanch asparagus in boiling water. Sauté blanched asparagus in oil, garlic, salt and pepper.

Sauté cooked rice with cream. Add butter and cheese, cook and stir until creamy. Diagonally slice tuna. Ladle sauce onto plate. Top with rice and asparagus. Place tuna slices on rice.

Wine Pairing:
Robert Mondavi — Merlot 'Private Selection'

Aris's Wine Notes: How can you look at the picture of this dish and not think "red wine"? We don't need a big red here, rather something tamer and softer to support and highlight the rich and complex flavors of the top grade components of this superbly crafted dish. Mondavi's Merlot has the consistency of style and quality with a firm grip on the soft texture and vibrant fruity nature of Merlot grape grown in the Central Coast vineyards.

4 (8-ounce) sashimi tuna fillets
1 cup sesame seed mix
vegetable oil
1 cup pineapple juice
⅓ cup soy sauce
⅓ cup rice wine vinegar
⅓ cup sesame oil
⅔ cup light brown sugar
2 teaspoons chopped chives
4 tablespoons sesame seed mix
1 teaspoon each salt and pepper
1 teaspoon ground ginger
12 stalks asparagus
extra virgin olive oil
1 clove garlic, minced
salt and pepper to taste
2 cups cooked rice
1 cup heavy cream
2 tablespoons butter, unsalted
4 tablespoons grated Romano
   cheese

Makes 4 servings

Thom's Tips: A perfect piece of tuna is bright red all over, inside and outside. While brown or gray is an okay color for tuna on the outside, it is not a good color for the inside.

Ahi Tuna with
Asian Sweet and Sour Soy Sauce

From: Vinnie's Steakhouse & Seafood • 7440 Six Forks Road • **Raleigh, NC 27615**

4 (5-ounce) sashimi grade
    tuna fillets
1 tablespoon white sesame seeds
1 tablespoon black sesame seeds
1 tablespoon extra virgin olive oil
1 tablespoon wasabi powder
1 tablespoon water
lemon, for garnish

Asian Sweet and Sour Sauce

1 cup Kikkoman's soy sauce
2 tablespoons honey
1 tablespoon pickled ginger
2 tablespoons orange marmalade
dash of red pepper flakes

Seaweed Salad

1 pound seaweed (goma wakame
    preferred)
1 tablespoon rice wine vinegar
1 tablespoon salt
1 tablespoon white sesame seeds

Makes 4 servings

Thom's Tips: Grades of tuna. A — Sushi. B — Grilling. C — the stuff you find in the can.

Coat fish with sesame seeds. Grill on all sides with olive oil until rare or to the desired temperature. Remove from heat. Let rest.

Mix wasabi and water together to form a paste. Set aside.

Thinly slice tuna. Arrange on plate with Seaweed Salad, side of Asian Sweet and Sour Sauce, wasabi and lemon.

Asian Sweet and Sour Sauce:

Mix soy sauce, honey, ginger, marmalade and red pepper flakes in a food processor. Pour into a bowl.

Seaweed Salad:

Chop seaweed finely. Mix together with vinegar, salt and white sesame seeds. Set aside.

Wine Pairing:
Dr. Fischer — Ockfener Bockstein Riesling Kabinett

Aris's Wine Notes: The soil of the Bockstein vineyard consists of hard slate stones. These stones help hold the sun's heat to warm the vine on the cold evenings and add a strong mineral component to the flavors. The wine has ripe apple and citrus fruit flavors that enliven the palate and marry with the tuna. The light sweetness and brisk acidity matches the sweet and sour Asian sauce.

Creole
Barbeque Shrimp

From: Cajun Queen • **1800 East 7th Street** • **Charlotte, NC 28204**

Heat a sauté pan and add oil. Add garlic, BBQ seasoning and Worcestershire sauce. Add shrimp and sauté until almost completely cooked. Add beer, chicken stock, onions and butter. Ready to serve.

Beer Pairing:
Spoetgl—Shiner Bock

Aris's Beer Notes: Spoetzl Brewery's Shiner Bock is renowned for its affinity for spicy Tex-Mex foods and so felt right at home with this Creole BBQ Shrimp. It is brewed to deliver a rich and velvety palate that soaks up the spicy heat.

1 teaspoon vegetable oil

1 teaspoon chopped garlic

1 teaspoon BBQ seasoning

3 teaspoons Worcestershire sauce

½ pound shrimp, peeled and
    deveined

¼ cup lager beer

½ cup chicken stock

¼ cup diced green onions

3 teaspoons butter

Makes 4 servings

Thom's Tips: To make this a truly fast dish, buy peeled shrimp at the grocery store. It may cost a little more, but it sure saves time. It usually takes me about 45 seconds per shrimp to peel them. I would much rather be eating them.

Inn at Brevard Crab Cakes and Roasted Red Pepper Coulis Sauce

From: Inn at Brevard • 410 East Main Street • Brevard, NC 28712

2 cups bay scallops

2 cups white lump crabmeat

salt and pepper to taste

1 teaspoon Tabasco

¼ cup sherry

1 teaspoon dry mustard

½ to 1 cup light mayonnaise

4 tablespoons breadcrumbs, panko
    preferred

3 eggs

½ cup chopped green onions

½ cup chopped Vidalia onions

1 tablespoon Old Bay seafood
    seasoning

2 tablespoons chopped flat-leaf
    parsley

1 cup seasoned flour

2 eggs, lightly beaten with
    1 tablespoon water

2 cups (or more) breadcrumbs,
    panko preferred

olive oil

1 (16-ounce) can roasted red peppers

salt and pepper

2 lemons, cut in half

Makes 4 servings

Thom's Tips: Crabmeat is expensive. Add puréed scallops to your crabmeat. This way you don't use as much crabmeat, but still have that great seafood taste.

Preheat oven to 400 degrees F.

Purée scallops in a blender. Mix together with crabmeat, salt, pepper, Tabasco, sherry, mustard, mayonnaise, breadcrumbs, eggs, onions, Old Bay and parsley. Make small crab cakes and form into patties. Dip in seasoned flour, then egg wash, then breadcrumbs. Sauté in olive oil until brown on both sides. Bake in oven for 8 minutes.

Put roasted red peppers in a blender and blend until smooth. Add salt and pepper to taste. Pour sauce into a saucepan. Place in oven to heat while cooking crab cakes.

To serve, put heated sauce on a dish with one or two crab cakes. Garnish with lemon.

<u>Wine Pairing:</u>
La Puerta — Torrontes

Aris's Wine Notes: La Puerta Torrontes is an extremely versatile wine, pairing nicely with food and yet easy to sip and enjoy on its own. Wines made from the Torrontes grape are quickly becoming the signature white wines of Argentina. The lovely floral and ripe fruit aromas with mineral notes are a delight.

Murrells Inlet Seafood Grits with Sausage

From: Divine Dining Group • 3993 Hwy 17 • Murrells Inlet, SC 29576

4 ounces pork fatback

1 large yellow onion, diced

4 stalks celery, diced

½ pound smoked sausage, diced

4 cloves garlic, peeled and chopped

1 cup dry white wine

2 bay leaves

1 (10-ounce) can clam juice

2 large ripe tomatoes

1 cup stone-ground grits

4 cups whole milk

2 tablespoons chopped fresh garlic

2 tablespoons butter

2 potatoes, diced

1 dozen littleneck clams, scrubbed

1 cup firm fresh fish (swordfish, mako shark, grouper, etc.), cut into 1-inch cubes

1 dozen live mussels, scrubbed and debearded

1 cup lobster meat

12 medium-sized shrimp, peeled and deveined

1 cup jumbo lump crab

1 cup shucked oysters

1 teaspoon chopped fresh parsley

2 lemons, cut in quarters

Makes 4 servings

Dice fatback into ¼-inch cubes. Heat a large pan. Add pork cubes, stirring frequently over medium heat. When pork is golden brown, add onion, celery, sausage and garlic and sauté for 2 to 3 minutes. Add wine and bay leaves; bring to a simmer. Add clam juice and simmer for 30 minutes.

Bring a medium-sized pot of water to a boil. Concassé tomatoes by plunging in boiling water for 20 seconds, then removing to ice water. Peel, squeeze seeds out, discard seeds and peel. Chop tomato into ¼-inch pieces. Set aside.

After base has simmered for 30 minutes, add tomato concassé. Remove from heat. This base may be kept refrigerated for up to 2 days.

Start grits in cold milk with chopped garlic. Stir occasionally and more frequently when just coming to a boil. Simmer for 45 minutes to 1 hour. When cooked, whisk in butter. Cover and set aside.

Boil potatoes in water until soft. Drain and set aside.

To finish dish, bring base to a simmer. Add clams and fish pieces; cover. Wait 2 minutes or until clams just begin to open. Add mussels, lobster, shrimp and potatoes and cover. Wait 2 minutes or until seafood boil is just simmering again. Add crabmeat and oysters; remove from heat.

Ladle grits into the bottom of 4 large bowls. Ladle seafood boil into the bowls and garnish with parsley and lemons.

Wine Pairing:
Pedroncelli — F. Johnson Vineyard Chardonnay

Aris's Wine Notes: This is a hearty dish that needs a hearty wine, a job perfectly suited to a classic California Chardonnay. There is just enough toasty, vanilla-laced oak to give complexity to the fruit and complement the smoky taste of the sausage.

Thom's Tips: Not only do I get to learn how to cook on this show, but I get to expand my vocabulary. Today's word is *concassé*. I have discovered that it is a fancy French term describing tomatoes that have been peeled, seeded and chopped into ¼-inch pieces.

Carolina "Low Country"
Seafood Paella

From: Arpa—Spanish Wine Bar/Tapas Bar • 121 West Trade Street • Charlotte, NC 28202

1½ dozen mussels, thoroughly
    cleansed

5½ cups fish broth or clam juice

¼ teaspoon crumbled thread saffron

¾ pound monkfish, cut into
    ½-inch pieces

¾ pound grouper, cut into ½-inch
    pieces

1 pound small cleaned squid with
    tentacles, cut into rounds

12 large fresh white shrimp in their
    shells

salt

2 tablespoons chopped parsley

8 cloves garlic, minced

1 tablespoon fresh thyme leaves

sea salt

2 teaspoons sweet paprika

8 tablespoons olive oil, divided

1 medium onion, finely chopped

6 small scallions, finely chopped

2 red bell peppers, finely chopped

1 medium tomato, finely chopped

3 cups Spanish rice

1½ dozen mussels, thoroughly
    cleansed

Makes 4 to 6 servings

Preheat your oven to 400 degrees F.

Place 1½ dozen mussels in a skillet with ¾ cup water. Cover and bring to a boil. Remove the mussels as they open. Reserve the meat and discard the shells. When all mussels have opened, pour the liquid from the skillet into a large pot. Add enough fish broth or clam juice to make 6 cups. Stir in the saffron. Keep the broth hot over the lowest heat.

Dry the monkfish, grouper, squid and shrimp. Sprinkle with salt. Let sit for 10 minutes at room temperature.

In a mortar, mash to a paste parsley, garlic, thyme and a pinch of sea salt. Stir in paprika. Add a little water if necessary to make a paste.

Heat 6 tablespoons of the oil in a paella pan (or in a shallow casserole dish) on top of your stove. Quickly sauté the monkfish, grouper, squid and shrimp for 1 to 2 minutes. Remove the seafood to a warm platter. Add the remaining oil, onion, scallions and bell peppers. Cook over medium-high heat until the vegetables are slightly softened. Raise the heat. Add the tomato and cook about 2 minutes.

Stir in the rice and coat well with the pan mixture. Pour in all the hot broth and bring to a boil. Continue to boil for 3 minutes, stirring and rotating the pan occasionally. Add all the reserved fish (except the shrimp), the reserved mussel meat, and the mortar mixture. Taste for salt. Continue to boil about 2 minutes more, until the rice is no longer soupy but sufficient liquid remains to continue cooking the rice.

Arrange the shrimp and the uncooked mussels on the rice. Place the edge of the mussel shells so that they will open face up. Transfer to the oven and cook, uncovered, until rice is almost done, 10 to 12 minutes. Remove to a warm spot and cover with foil. Let rest for 10 minutes.

Thom's Tips: Time for the Spanish word of the day: paella. Paella is a rice dish that comes from the region of Valencia in Spain. Its main ingredients are rice, saffron and olive oil. From those three ingredients chefs add various seafood, vegetables and meats.

Wine Pairing:
Robert Mondavi — Fume Blanc

Aris's Wine Notes: This style of Sauvignon is dry, crisp and refreshing with vibrant fruit tasting of citrus, pineapple and lemongrass with notes of gooseberry, green herbs and minerals. A dash of Semillon adds roundness and notes of melon and fig while a hiss of oak lends a touch of vanilla. It takes a versatile wine to deal with an 'everything but the kitchen sink' dish like this and the wine performs admirably.

Pan-Seared Scallops over Creamed Corn with Balsamic Syrup, Parmesan Crisp and Garlic Foam

From: Mr. Friendly's New Southern Cafe • 2001-A Greene Street • Columbia, SC 29205

12 jumbo sea scallops (dry packed), side muscle removed

salt and pepper

olive oil or butter for sautéing

1 cup balsamic vinegar

1 to 2 ears sweet corn, shucked

2 tablespoons diced onion

1 clove garlic, minced

½ cup white wine

1 teaspoon fresh thyme

½ cup cream

1 tablespoon grated Parmesan, per crisp

1 tablespoon roasted garlic

½ cup chilled heavy cream

Makes 4 servings

Thom's Tips: Dry-packed sea scallops are simply frozen until they arrive at your store. Trust me: these are the scallops you want. Wet-packed scallops are packed in sodium tripolyphosphate (STP). Other than being a scary chemical name, the STP will cause the scallops to absorb water like a sponge. Not only are you paying for water instead of scallops, when you cook the scallops they will release the absorbed water, leaving you with rubbery shrunken scallops.

Preheat oven to 350 degrees F.

Season scallops with salt and pepper. Sear on both sides in a sauté pan with oil or butter, flipping when golden brown.

Pour balsamic vinegar in a saucepan and reduce over medium-high heat until syrup consistency.

Cut corn off the cob. Sauté onion and garlic with butter. Add corn and sauté. Deglaze with wine and then add thyme, salt and pepper. Add cream and allow to thicken; remove from heat.

On baking tray, place aluminum foil and spray with cooking spray. Take a tablespoon of Parmesan cheese and spread it out on the aluminum foil. Bake in oven until the cheese melts and turns slightly brown, approximately 7 to 9 minutes. Remove from oven.

Using a hand mixer, mix garlic, heavy cream and salt and pepper into a creamy froth.

Ladle corn onto a plate and then place 2 to 3 scallops on corn. Add Parmesan crisps and a dollop of garlic cream to the plate.

Wine Pairing:
Mia's Playground — Chardonnay

Aris's Wine Notes: Scallops are delicate and sweet, with subtle flavors. In this dish, we have to contend with the strong and sharp flavors of the balsamic and the Parmesan. Feeling I needed a full-throttle Chardonnay, I chose Mia's Playground. The palate bursts with luscious fig and tropical fruits and finishes like lemon-zested vanilla cream. There is just enough acidity to tie the package together.

Fried Coconut Shrimp over Wasabi Slaw and a Sweet and Sour Chili Glaze

From: Crescent Grill • 1035 Broad Street • Camden, SC 29020

Score your shrimp on the diagonal on the bottoms. Mix together flour, soda water, salt, vinegar and cornstarch. Mix together breadcrumbs and coconut.

Holding the shrimp by the tail, dip it into the batter. Then dip into the breadcrumb and coconut mixture.

Make sure your breaded shrimp is straight. Drop into a 350-degree fryer and cook until it floats.

Chop cabbage into thin strips.

Toast the sesame seeds.

In a mixing bowl, add the wasabi powder mix in hot water until creamy. Add lemon juice and soy sauce. Add a pinch of salt and pepper. Mix in mayonnaise. Toss together with cabbage and sesame seeds.

Add the vinegar and sugar into a small sauce pot with the Thai chile, garlic and scallions. Let the mixture reduce for about 20 minutes or until it coats the back of a spoon. Add the cilantro.

Serve by placing the wasabi slaw on the plate. Place four fried shrimp on top of the slaw. Drizzle sweet and sour chili glaze on plate and shrimp.

Wine Pairing:
Murphy-Goode — Fume Blanc

Aris's Wine Notes: I love Sauvignon Blanc with shellfish and felt that this dish, with its reliance on heat from the wasabi and chili, needed more fruit and textural richness for balance. Murphy-Goode is a master at crafting Sauvignon Blanc in the style I needed. Lush tropical fruits with melon and fig overtones are given an extra measure of richness by the addition of some barrel-fermented wine, which also adds hints of smoke and vanilla.

12 (16/20 count) shrimp, peeled with tail on

2 cups all-purpose flour

3 cups soda water

1 tablespoon salt

2 tablespoons rice wine vinegar

½ cup cornstarch

3 cups breadcrumbs, panko preferred

3 cups shredded coconut

1 head cabbage

2 tablespoons sesame seeds

4 tablespoons wasabi powder

4 tablespoons hot water

1 tablespoon lemon juice

1 tablespoon soy sauce

salt and pepper to taste

2 cups mayonnaise

3 cups rice wine vinegar

3 cups sugar

1 tablespoon Thai chile

4 cloves garlic, chopped

1 bunch scallions, thinly sliced

1 bunch cilantro, chopped

Makes 4 servings

Thom's Tips: One of my favorite ways to tell if something is done in a deep fryer is when it floats. Granted, not everything floats, but as a good rule of thumb if it pops up to the top it is probably done.

Cajun-Fried Eggplant
with Seafood Medley

From: Cafe on the Square • One Biltmore Avenue • Asheville, NC 28801

8 eggplant slices, peeled and sliced
  ¼ inch

2 eggs, beaten

2 cups breadcrumbs

Cajun seasoning

1 cup olive oil, for frying

12 shrimp, peeled

1 cup crawfish meat

12 bay scallops

1 cup sliced andouille sausage

1 cup thinly sliced green
  bell peppers

1 cup chopped red onion

1 cup chopped portobello
  mushrooms

salt and pepper

4 teaspoons Tabasco

2 teaspoons Cajun seasoning

1 teaspoon fresh tarragon

1 cup cooking sherry

1 cup heavy cream

3 tablespoons butter

1 bunch asparagus

Makes 4 servings

Thom's Tips: I like to change the recipes slightly. In this case, chicken can also be used in addition to or instead of any of the main ingredients.

Dip eggplant slices in egg. Cover with breadcrumbs and sprinkle with Cajun seasoning. Heat olive oil in a saucepan. Fry eggplant until golden brown on both sides. Remove from pan and place on paper towels.

Sauté shrimp, crawfish, scallops, sausage, bell peppers, onion and mushrooms in olive oil. Season with salt and pepper. Add Tabasco sauce, Cajun seasoning and tarragon. Deglaze pan with sherry. Add heavy cream and butter. Reduce until thick.

Bring water to a boil and blanch asparagus; remove asparagus and place in ice water.

Ladle seafood and vegetables into a bowl. Place two eggplant slices and asparagus on top.

<u>Wine Pairing:</u>
Smoking Loon — Syrah

Aris's Wine Notes: Pairing a red with this dish was a stretch, but I felt the eggplant, sausage, peppers and mushrooms would dominate the seafood, thus calling for a red wine. With the Smoking Loon Syrah, the flavors burst through with intense blueberry and strawberry jam notes wrapped around rich French oak and finishing with touches of milk chocolate, sweetened cranberries and savory herbs. You could also pair an amber beer with this dish.

Curried Crab and Goat Cheese Soufflé

From: 700 Cooking School—Mansion on Forsyth Park • 700 Drayton Street • Savannah, GA 31401

1 tablespoon olive oil

1 tablespoon butter

2 tablespoons finely minced shallots

1 tablespoon finely diced red bell pepper

¼ teaspoon curry powder

pinch of cayenne pepper

2 tablespoons all-purpose flour

1¼ cups half-and-half

¾ cup crumbled goat cheese

1 tablespoon minced fresh dill

2 tablespoons sherry

1 cup lump crabmeat (remove any bits of shell)

6 egg whites, room temperature

pinch of cream of tartar

pinch of salt

For Soufflé dishes

4 tablespoons butter, softened

¾ cup finely ground breadcrumbs

Makes 4 to 6 servings

Preheat oven to 400 degrees F.

Heat olive oil and butter in a small saucepan over medium heat. Allow butter to melt. Add shallots and bell pepper and sauté. Add curry powder and cayenne pepper and continue to cook. Toast the spices over medium-low heat for about 1 minute; do not let vegetables brown. Sprinkle flour over vegetable mixture. Cook over medium heat for about 1 to 2 minutes. Using a whisk, stir in the half-and-half. Whisk and cook until mixture is thickened, about 2 to 3 minutes. Add the goat cheese and whisk to blend in the cheese as it melts. Remove pan from heat and stir in the dill and sherry until blended. Pour into a 3-quart mixing bowl and allow mixture to cool down to room temperature.

Prepare soufflé dishes by buttering with softened butter and coating with breadcrumbs. Once mixture is at room temperature, fold in the crabmeat and set aside.

Place egg whites into the large bowl of an electric mixer or a 3-quart stainless or glass bowl if using an electric hand mixer. Add a pinch of cream of tartar and a pinch of salt to the egg whites. Begin whipping on low speed until mixture begins to get frothy and foamy. Turn speed up to medium-high and whip until soft peaks form and finally turn up once more to high speed. Whip egg whites until they form stiff peaks.

Add a quarter of the egg whites to the soufflé base and stir in to lighten the consistency. Add one-half of the remaining egg whites and gently fold into the base. It is not necessary to completely blend them at this point, as the remaining whites still need to be added. Add remaining egg whites and fold into the base. When all of the egg whites have been folded in, divide mixture between the soufflé dishes,

filling each one to about ½-inch from the top. Smooth the tops of each soufflé and place on a baking sheet.

Place into the preheated oven and bake for 12 minutes. The soufflés are done when they have risen above the top edge of the dish and have a very tiny jiggle at the center. Using tongs, remove from baking tray and place on small plates. Serve immediately.

Wine Pairing:
Dirler — Riesling Bollenberg

Aris's Wine Notes: A lovely wine that delivers an enticing bouquet of honeysuckle and citrus with stony mineral scents. There's a sense of youthful vitality, elegance and class, yet it has the depth and structure to slice through food like a finely honed knife. It refreshes the palate and blends its flavors with the dish for an exciting finale. Neither the richness of the cheese nor the spiciness of the curry gave the wine any problems.

Thom's Tips: The mixture can be prepared up to two days in advance. If preparing in advance, allow the mixture to cool to room temperature, then place plastic wrap tightly against the surface of the base. This will prevent it from forming a "skin" on top.

Shrimp and Blue Crab Crêpes

From: Chelsea's Wine Bar & Eatery • One South Front Street • Wilmington, NC 28401

¼ cup butter, melted
2 teaspoons minced shallot
1 teaspoon minced garlic
1 pound large shrimp, peeled and
    deveined
¼ cup dry white wine
½ teaspoon dry dill weed
½ pound lump crabmeat
1 tablespoon minced chives, plus
    1 tablespoon for garnish
½ cup Boursin cheese
2 (6-inch) crêpes, per guest
chives
black pepper

Cream Sauce

½ pound unsalted butter, softened
1½ cups sour cream
¼ cup cream cheese, softened
1 teaspoon salt

Red Pepper Vinaigrette

1 (14-ounce) can fire-roasted red
    bell peppers
1 cup champagne vinegar
1 teaspoon granulated garlic
1 teaspoon dry thyme
½ teaspoon crushed red chili flakes
1 cup olive oil
salt and pepper

Makes 4 servings

Preheat oven to 350 degrees F.

Heat sauté pan over medium-high heat and melt butter. Sauté shallots until tender, about 3 minutes. Add garlic and cook about 2 minutes. Add shrimp and cook until pink. Pour in the wine and add the dill and cook about 4 minutes. Transfer shrimp to a pan to cool completely. Once cool, roughly chop the shrimp and place in a bowl. Mix in crabmeat, chives and Boursin. Divide the mix evenly between the crêpes. Place the mix closer to one end of the crepe. Roll the crêpe over the mix. Wrap crêpes (two per person) in aluminum foil and heat in the oven for about 6 minutes. Take crêpes out of the oven, unwrap and cut in half. Top crêpes with Cream Sauce, Red Pepper Vinaigrette, chives and black pepper.

Cream Sauce:

Place all ingredients in a mixer with a whisk attachment. Whip until all blended and smooth.

Red Pepper Vinaigrette:

Roughly chop peppers and place in a processor. Add vinegar, garlic, thyme and chili flakes. Process until smooth. Slowly add oil until completely emulsified. Adjust seasonings with salt and pepper to taste.

Wine Pairing:
McManis — Viognier

Aris's Wine Notes: We looked for a wine that was a rich array of fruit flavors yet firmly structured and without oak influences to match this elegant dish. Viognier, as made in California, yields just such a wine and McManis makes a surprisingly crisp version. Honeysuckle and apricot with notes of pear and grapefruit blend well with the delicate fish flavors. Another great thing about McManis wines is getting good quality at a fair price.

Thom's Tips: In a hurry? Want to make crepes but don't want to spend time waiting for the batter to settle? Buy them pre-made from your local grocery store. They come just like tortillas. Just reheat them and take all the credit for the perfect crepes.

Rock Shrimp
Risotto

From: The Plantation Room at Celebration Hotel • 700 Bloom Street • Celebration, FL 34747

Shrimp Stock

¼ pound shrimp shells

½ onion, chopped

1 stalk celery, chopped

½ carrot, chopped

1 bay leaf

2 quarts water

1 tomato, chopped

¼ cup olive oil

2 tablespoons chopped shallots

6 cups risotto rice

salt and pepper to taste

½ cup white wine

2 quarts Shrimp Stock

1 cup heavy whipping cream

1 pound rock shrimp, peeled

2 tablespoons chopped fresh basil

½ cup grated Parmesan cheese

½ cup grated Romano cheese

Makes 4 servings

Thom's Tips: Having you own personal cooking stocks gives your food a rich and unique taste. Use veal bones, chicken leftovers, shrimp shells—just add vegetables and boil. Store in the refrigerator or put in the freezer for later use.

Shrimp Stock

To create the Shrimp Stock, place all ingredients in large saucepan and bring to boil. Turn the stock down and simmer for 10 minutes. Strain the stock and set aside.

Use a medium saucepan and heat the olive oil. Add shallots and sweat until clear in color, making sure not to burn. Add rice and then season with salt and pepper. While stirring the rice, deglaze the pan with wine and ¼ of the Shrimp Stock. Allow the rice to cook slowly, adding a little stock at a time. Add remaining stock and then cream. Let the rice cook until slightly tender to the tooth. Add shrimp and basil. Cover tightly with a lid. Turn off the heat and let the rice sit for 2 minutes.

Serve the rice with a little Parmesan or Romano cheese for garnish.

Wine Pairing:
Rudi Wiest Selection — Mosel River Riesling

Aris's Wine Notes: This a very rich and creamy dish yet delicately flavored, very subtle and quietly complex. There is one wine that matches those qualities and that wine is German Riesling. The wine delivers a lively, blossomy nose of honeysuckle and lemon.

Moroccan Pesto
Calamari

From: 95 Cordova • **95 Cordova Street** • **St. Augustine, FL 32084**

Heat about 4 inches of oil in a large pot to 400 degrees F.

Wash and dry calamari with a clean kitchen towel. Mix together cornmeal and flour in a bowl. Add calamari; this is best done in batches. Place flour-coated calamari in a sieve and shake to remove excess flour. Place in hot oil and cook until just golden, about 30 seconds and floating in the oil. Remove from oil with a slotted spoon to drain on paper towels; keep warm.

Set on plate and cover with Moroccan Pesto Sauce. Sprinkle with olives, cheese, tomatoes and cilantro.

Moroccan Pesto Sauce:

Mix together cumin, curry powder, coriander, sugar, hot sauce and mayonnaise. Set aside.

Wine Pairing:
Foley — Santa Rita Hills 'Rancho Santa Rosa' Chardonnay

Aris's Wine Notes: This fabulous dish is richly textured and packed with flavorful spices, but is not hot spicy. We wanted a wine that would make an equally bold statement as the dish and chose a Chardonnay. The aroma is a tightly integrated blend of crisp Chardonnay fruit; a butter-scotch richness; sweet, toasty oak and hints of yeast and minerals. A delightful package, eminently suited to this dish.

vegetable oil for frying
1 pound cleaned calamari rings
   and tentacles
½ cup cornmeal
½ cup flour
1 cup kalamata olives, pitted and
   sliced
1 cup stuffed green olives, sliced
1 cup grated Asiago cheese
1 cup diced tomatoes
2 tablespoons chopped fresh
   cilantro

Moroccan Pesto Sauce
2 tablespoons ground cumin
2 tablespoons curry powder
1 tablespoon ground coriander
2 tablespoons brown sugar
1 tablespoon Louisiana Hot Sauce
2 cups mayonnaise

Makes 4 to 6 servings

Thom's Tips: It is important when blotting dry seafood that you use a towel that does not shed. Paper towels will fall apart or get caught on the seafood and terry cloth towels drop lots of lint. Any residue will end up getting fried with the food.

Crab Cakes with Remoulade Sauce

From: City Tavern Hearst Tower • 215 South Tryon, Suite D • Charlotte, NC 28202

1 pound crabmeat

½ cup sliced scallions

1 cup grated Parmesan cheese

½ cup diced red bell peppers

¾ cup breadcrumbs

1 teaspoon cayenne pepper

1 teaspoon garlic, chopped

½ teaspoon salt

½ teaspoon pepper

6 ounces cooked angel hair pasta

2 whole eggs, beaten well

olive and canola oils

1 bulb jicama, peeled and diced
    ¼ inch

1 red bell pepper, deseeded and
    diced ¼ inch

1 green bell pepper, deseeded and
    diced ¼ inch

¼ red onion, finely chopped

¾ cup red wine vinegar

⅓ cup olive oil

½ teaspoon chopped garlic

1 teaspoon salt and pepper mix

1 cup capers

1 tablespoon lemon juice

¾ cup ketchup

3 cups mayonnaise

½ teaspoon cayenne pepper

Makes 4 servings

In a mixing bowl combine crabmeat, scallions, cheese, bell peppers, breadcrumbs, cayenne pepper, garlic, salt and pepper; toss well.

In a separate bowl, toss pasta with eggs. Combine egg-coated pasta with crab mixture. Make sure to not break up pasta. Form small patties. Crab cakes should have pasta coming out of them for a spidery look when fried. Fry in an olive oil and canola oil blend. Set aside on paper towels.

Toss together jicama, bell peppers, onion, vinegar, olive oil and garlic; season to taste. Set aside in refrigerator.

Purée capers and lemon juice in a food processor until smooth. Remove into mixing bowl. Add ketchup, mayonnaise and cayenne pepper. Whisk until smooth.

Serve two crab cakes with jicama salsa and remoulade.

Wine Pairing:
Yellowtail — Reserve Pinot Grigio

Aris's Wine Notes: Pinot Gris is a good choice for wines in the lower price brackets, as it often delivers more interesting flavors than Chardonnay. There is a "fruit basket" quality to the flavors, making it hard to focus in on just one fruit analogy. There is just enough acidity to handle food, but not enough to feel tart.

Poultry & Fowl

Pecan-Encrusted
Chicken

From: Cafe on the Square • One Biltmore Avenue • Asheville, NC 28801

2 cups wild rice

2¾ cups water

1 tablespoon butter

2 tablespoons seasoning (blend of pepper, powdered onion, salt, basil, oregano)

1 tablespoon sesame oil

2 tablespoons soybean oil

1 tablespoon chopped garlic

1 teaspoon coarse black pepper

4 (8-ounce) chicken breasts

1 cup panko (Japanese breadcrumbs)

1 cup shelled pecan pieces

1 tablespoon ground coriander

1 teaspoon coarse black pepper

1 teaspoon kosher salt

2 teaspoons onion powder

Whiskey Dijon

1 cup honey

½ cup coarse ground Dijon

2 tablespoons cider vinegar

1 tablespoon cumin

1 ounce bourbon

Makes 4 servings

Thom's Tips: On *Carolina Cooking,* we put just about anything in a food processor. The best way to get an even consistency is to pulse the food processor and let ingredients nearly come to a rest between pulses.

Preheat oven to 350 degrees F.

Mix rice, water, butter and seasonings. Cover with aluminum foil. Put in oven and bake for 20 minutes.

Mix together sesame oil, soybean oil, garlic and pepper. Add chicken breasts to marinate.

Pureé breadcrumbs and pecans in a food processor until pecans are almost fine but still have some nutty texture. Stir in coriander, pepper, salt and onion powder. Dredge chicken in the pecan breading mixture and press. Heat flat griddle or sauté pan over medium-low heat. Add cooking oil infused with sesame oil and brown. Cook on stove top until chicken is completely cooked through center. (Note: If chicken browns too quickly, turn down heat or finish in the oven at 350 degrees F.)

To serve, pour Whiskey Dijon over rice and chicken.

Whiskey Dijon:

Make Whiskey Dijon sauce while chicken is cooking. Whisk all ingredients together and set aside.

Wine Pairing:
MacMurray Ranch — Pinot Noir

Aris's Wine Notes: MacMurray Ranch focuses on Pinot Noir as its only red. This is a full-throttle Pinot Noir, fully capable of handling this dish with its wide array of spices without overwhelming it like a Cabernet or Syrah probably would. Plush black cherry and plum fruit spiced with a touch of sage and vanilla ride on a supple palate that has a solid backbone but never feels sharp or astringent.

Chicken Topped
with Crawfish Diane

From: Cajun Queen • **1800 East 7th Street** • **Charlotte, NC 28204**

Preheat oven to 350 degrees F.

Dredge chicken breasts in flour. Heat oil in sauté pan. Add chicken and cook until golden; flip. When other side is golden brown, put chicken in oven and bake to desired temperature.

To the sauté pan add garlic, Diane seasoning, mushrooms and crawfish. Sauté for about 1 minute. Deglaze pan with chicken stock. Add butter and let melt. Add parsley and green onions and then remove from heat.

Place chicken on plate. Ladle crawfish sauce over chicken.

Wine Pairing:
Robert Mondavi —— Chardonnay

Aris's Wine Notes: Like all Mondavi estate wines, this Chardonnay is classic in all respects. This is a carefully proportioned wine of charm, balance and power and great flexibility at the table. The dish needed a wine of substance to handle the chicken and the spicy sauce, but with the proper restraint to not overshadow its unique array of flavors.

4 (8- to 10-ounce) chicken breasts
1 cup all-purpose flour
¼ cup cooking oil
1 tablespoon chopped garlic
2 teaspoons Cajun Queen Diane
   seasoning
 4 cups sliced mushrooms
1 cup crawfish tail meat
1½ cups chicken stock
2 tablespoons butter
1 tablespoon chopped parsley
½ cup diced green onions

Makes 4 servings

Thom's Tips: I used to think that "deglaze" was just a fancy French cooking word to throw the novice off. I have since discovered that deglazing a pan with wine, stock or water is an easy way to capture meat juices and flavors that have stuck to the pan. You can turn what you would normally spend 20 minutes scrubbing off into a yummy sauce for the dish you are preparing.

Ginger-Roasted Chicken with Green Beans

From: Jujube Restaurant-Asian Kitchen and Bar • 1201-L Raleigh Road • Chapel Hill, NC 27514

½ cup ginger, peeled and roughly chopped

2 cups boiling water

⅓ cup brown sugar

½ cup kosher salt

⅓ cup sweet chili

3 tablespoons fish sauce

7 cups ice water

3 pounds chicken pieces

1 pound green beans, cleaned

2 teaspoons peanut oil

2 cloves garlic, thinly sliced

1 tablespoon soy sauce

oil, for frying

1 tablespoon finely chopped ginger

2 tablespoons Basic Spicy Dressing (see below)

Shallot Nectarine Compote (see next page)

Basic Spicy Dressing

1 cup fish sauce

1½ cups sweet chili

1 cup lime juice

½ cup rice vinegar

Preheat oven to 400 degrees F.

Add the chopped ginger to the boiling water and allow to steep for 15 minutes. Place in a large container. Mix in the sugar, salt, chili and fish sauce and stir to dissolve. Add ice water and then the chicken. Cure for at least 8 hours.

Bring a large pot of salted water to a rapid boil. Make an ice bath in a large bowl. Blanch the beans for about 30 seconds, then plunge them into the ice bath. Drain and set aside.

Heat peanut oil in a large sauté pan and cook the garlic until golden. Add in the beans and the soy sauce and toss well. Set aside.

After allowing chicken to cure, remove from brine and let drain on a wire rack in the refrigerator. Blot the chicken dry with paper towels. Heat oil to very hot in an oven-safe sauté pan, and sear chicken skin side down until browned. Turn the chicken over in the pan and place in the oven for 15 minutes (time will vary based on size of chicken pieces). Check beneath tender flap on breast for doneness. Take the pan out of the oven and remove the chicken. Add the chopped ginger to pan and deglaze with the Basic Spicy Dressing. Toss chicken in pan to coat and serve over Shallot Nectarine Compote with green beans.

Basic Spicy Dressing: Mix all ingredients together. Save extra for salad dressing or as sauce for meats.

Shallot Nectarine Compote: Heat the peanut oil in a heavy stainless steel pot over medium heat. Cook the shallots in the oil until caramelized and cover if necessary. After the shallots have caramelized, add the Shaoxing and nectarines. Toss to coat thoroughly.

Wine Pairing:
Cakebread — Chardonnay

Aris's Wine Notes: Cakebread Chardonnay is a lesson in balance, complexity and food compatibility. The palate is filled with ripe apple, pear and peach fruit brightened with citrus and mineral notes. Toasty oak and light yeast notes marry nicely with the fruit to complete the package. This lovely Chardonnay meets the ginger in the chicken and the nectarines in the compote to give an explosion of new flavors.

Shallot Nectarine Compote

1 teaspoon peanut oil

5 shallots, peeled and thickly sliced

1 tablespoon Shaoxing cooking wine

2 nectarines, sliced

Makes 4 servings

Thom's Tips: Shock your green veggies. Just take a pot of boiling water and dump in your green beans or asparagus for only about 15 to 20 seconds. Then take them out and put them in a bowl of ice water. It makes them green, cooked but still crisp.

Pollo al Marche

From: 700 Cooking School—Mansion on Forsyth Park • 700 Drayton Street • Savannah, GA 31401

3 tablespoons olive oil

2 medium onions, julienne sliced

⅔ cup grated Parmesan cheese

1 tablespoon minced fresh basil

zest and juice of 2 lemons

½ cup pimiento-stuffed green olives, coarsely chopped

¼ teaspoon black pepper

6 large boneless, skinless chicken breasts

¼ cup olive oil

1 tablespoon minced garlic

Lemon-Olive Vinaigrette

¾ cup extra virgin olive oil

3 basil leaves, crushed and bruised

2 cloves garlic, sliced in half lengthwise

½ cup lemon juice

salt and pepper

¼ cup pimiento-stuffed green olives, coarsely chopped

zest of 1 lemon

Makes 6 servings

Heat olive oil in a medium-size sauté pan. Add onions and sauté until caramelized, shaking often to keep from sticking as they begin to caramelize. This will take about 15 minutes. When onions have caramelized sufficiently, remove from heat and spread on a plate and refrigerate until cool to touch.

Place cooled onions, cheese, basil, lemon zest and juice, green olives and pepper in a 3-quart mixing bowl. Mix well to blend items and taste for seasoning. Adjust taste with more salt and pepper if necessary. Set aside.

Place chicken breasts on cutting board with the curved side of the breast up near the edge of the board closest to you. Using a boning knife or paring knife, cut a 3-inch long incision starting at the wider end of the breast and cut toward the narrow end. You want to create a "pocket" for the filling. Divide filling evenly between the chicken breasts and stuff each breast, pushing filling in evenly along length of chicken breast. Place chicken breasts on a baking sheet or large plate and drizzle with olive oil and rub with minced garlic. Season with salt and black pepper.

Place chicken on a preheated "medium-high" grill. Cook for about 5 minutes per side. Be careful not to overcook and dry out chicken. Serve with warm Lemon-Olive Vinaigrette drizzled over the top.

Lemon-Olive Vinaigrette: Place olive oil, basil and garlic in a small sauté pan. Place oil mixture over moderately-low heat for about 10 to 15 minutes so that flavors will infuse into the oil. Watch carefully so that basil and garlic do not brown or burn. Using a slotted spoon, remove garlic and basil from oil. Place lemon juice in a small non-reactive

bowl. Add a pinch of salt and some freshly ground black pepper. Drizzle oil into juice in a steady stream, whisking quickly. Add olives and lemon zest and return to sauté pan. Heat until hot. Drizzle over grilled chicken.

Wine Pairing:

Flora Springs — Soliloquy

Aris's Wine Notes: A soliloquy is a dramatic monologue, and this wine expresses its 100% Sauvignon Blanc heritage for all to hear, loud and clear. With a solid body and firm acidity, it is ready to challenge this rich and complex dish. It handles the chicken with ease, marries its flavors with the vegetables and has the acidity for the vinaigrette.

Thom's Tips: When cutting a pocket in chicken, keep your knife parallel with the cutting board. This helps you to avoid cutting through the bottom or top of the breast.

Chicken Milanese

From: Mia Famiglia • 19918 North Cove Road • Cornelius, NC 28031

4 (8-ounce) chicken breasts

flour

4 eggs, beaten

2 cups seasoned breadcrumbs

2 cups olive oil, divided

½ cup grated Parmesan cheese

8 (¼-inch) slices large ripe tomato

8 large basil leaves

1 pound fresh mozzarella, sliced

4 Yukon gold potatoes, ¼-inch slices

½ cup breadcrumbs

2 tablespoons minced garlic

2 tablespoons chopped fresh parsley

1 bunch fresh asparagus

½ stick butter

2 lemons, juiced

salt and pepper

⅛ cup sherry vinegar

Makes 4 servings

Thom's Tips: Because chicken breasts are a little thicker on one side, it is a good idea to lightly pound the thicker side so that the breasts become a uniform thickness. This way the chicken breasts will cook evenly. To pound, just wrap the chicken breast in plastic wrap and use a meat mallet. If you don't have a tenderizing mallet, improvise. I've used everything from a framing hammer wrapped in cellophane to an empty wine bottle.

Preheat oven to 400 degrees F.

Slice each chicken breast horizontally into two pieces. Lay the chicken flat on a cutting board. Cover the chicken with plastic wrap and pound with a meat mallet (or back of a frying pan). Dredge each piece in flour then in the egg wash, then in the breadcrumbs. Place about ¼ inch of oil into a large frying pan over medium heat. Fry the chicken until golden brown. Remove from the oil and sprinkle with Parmesan cheese. Place one slice of tomato, one basil leaf, and one slice of fresh mozzarella on top of each chicken breast. Place in oven for 3 to 4 minutes, or until the mozzarella is slightly melted.

Toss potatoes with breadcrumbs, garlic, parsley and ¼ cup olive oil. Lay out the potatoes flat on a sheet tray and bake for 25 minutes.

Drop asparagus into boiling water for 45 seconds. Remove from water and drop into an ice bath. In a sauté pan, melt butter then add juice of 1 lemon, pinch of salt and pepper over low heat. Add blanched asparagus and sauté for 3 to 4 minutes.

In a bowl, whisk together ½ cup olive oil, juice of 1 lemon, sherry, pinch of salt and pepper. Drizzle about ½ tablespoon over each piece of chicken. Serve with potatoes and asparagus.

Wine Pairing:
Greg Norman — Cabernet Merlot

Aris's Wine Notes: While chicken can often pair with red or white, the strong influences of the tomato, cheese and basil bring this into red wine country. The smooth tannins help prevent the wine from overwhelming the chicken or clashing with the acidity of the tomato.

Tamales with
Adobo Chicken

From: Salsa Mexican Caribbean Restaurant • 6 Patton Avenue • Asheville, NC 28801

6 ancho peppers

1 tablespoon cumin

2 tablespoons honey

1 tablespoon salt

1 teaspoon cinnamon

¼ cup olive oil

4 (8-ounce) chicken breasts

¼ cup sweet vinegar

2 cups masa (corn) flour

¾ cup warm water

1 tablespoon salt

1 tablespoon annatto seed

½ cup olive oil

12 corn husks

Mole Negro

1 poblano pepper

2 corn tortillas

½ cup almonds

½ cup sesame seeds

1 stick salted butter

7 mulato peppers

¼ cup black raisins

½ tablespoon salt

¼ cup chopped semisweet chocolate

4 star anise

1 cup chicken stock

1 tablespoon annatto powder

Preheat your grill.

Put the ancho peppers in very hot water for 5 minutes, or until they are soft. Remove from water. Remove seeds and stems. Add cumin, honey, salt, cinnamon and olive oil. Transfer to blender and blend until smooth.

Put chicken in a large bowl. Add vinegar and mix well. Pour blender marinade over chicken. Let stand in the fridge for a couple of hours. Grill chicken until done, 2 to 3 minutes each side. Cut into 2-inch strips.

In a bowl, combine masa, water and salt. Mix together.

In a separate pan, heat annatto and olive oil until it turns red. Pour oil mixture into masa and combine until a smooth consistency is reached. (Note: You may need to add more water.) Form into 2-inch balls and put in a tortilla press. To keep the dough from sticking to the press, place plastic wrap on both sides of the press. Press into round, thin corn cakes. Remove from press.

Place masa into corn husks. Add chicken on top of the masa and fold masa over chicken, then fold corn husk around masa. Steam the tamale for 10 minutes. Serve either with or without corn husks with Mole Negro and Corn and Chayote Mushroom Salsa.

Mole Negro:

Roast poblano pepper over fire or broil until the skin is burnt and peeling off. Remove from heat. Place in brown paper bag to cool. Remove from bag and peel off skin when cool.

Toast corn tortillas until slightly charred.

In a pan, add almonds and sesame seeds. Cook until dark. Add butter. Quickly add mulato peppers, raisins, salt,

chocolate, star anise, chicken stock and annatto. Cook until it boils, then transfer to blender. Add poblano pepper and tortillas and blend until smooth.

Corn and Chayote Mushroom Salsa:

Boil corn, mushroom and chayote for 5 minutes. In another pan, toast poppy seeds until they jump around in the pan, about 1 to 2 minutes. Remove corn mixture from pan and dice finely; add remaining ingredients. Mix well.

Wine Pairing:
Treana — Mer Soleil Vineyard White

Aris's Wine Notes: The unique blend of the Rhone Valley grapes, Viognier and Marsanne, are perfectly suited to each other. Viognier brings floral notes and tropical fruits, while Marsanne brings honey and minerals and solidity. Together, they deal with all aspects of the multitude of flavors this dish offers.

Corn & Chayote Mushroom Salsa

1 ear corn

1 portobello mushroom

1 chayote

1 teaspoon poppy seeds

2 tablespoons rice vinegar

1 teaspoon salt

¼ cup cilantro

1 tomato

2 tablespoons olive oil

Makes 4 to 6 servings

Thom's Tips: Now that you have the basic tamale recipe, go crazy. You can stuff the corn husk wrapper masa-filled pouch with cheese, meats, sweets and sours. The sky is the limit.

Buttermilk-Fried Duckling Breast over Thelma's Corn Fritters, Kale and Cherry Gastrique

From: Motor Supply Company Bistro • 920 Gervais Street • Columbia, SC 29209

4 duck breasts

1 teaspoon salt

1 teaspoon pepper

1 cup all-purpose flour

1 cup buttermilk

3 cups corn oil

3 eggs, separated

½ teaspoon salt

⅛ teaspoon fresh ground pepper

¼ cup all-purpose flour

1 ⅔ cups cooked corn

oil, for frying

1 teaspoon chopped garlic

3 tablespoons butter

1 bunch kale, chopped

5 tablespoons water

1 cup sugar

1 shallot, sliced

½ cup rice wine vinegar

¼ cup dried cherries

salt and pepper to taste

Makes 4 servings

Thom's Tips: Duck usually has a large layer of fat under its skin. This means that if you are frying the duck, you only need enough oil to keep the skin from sticking to the pan. As the duck cooks, the fat will melt, which will further fry the duck. This will keep the duck from tasting overly greasy.

Season duck with salt and pepper. Dredge duck in flour, then buttermilk, then back in the flour. Fry duck in corn oil until golden brown. Flip if needed.

Separate eggs. Beat egg yolks well and sift in salt, pepper and flour. Add corn and mix well. In a separate bowl beat egg whites to stiff peaks. Fold egg whites into the yolk mixture. Pan fry in small batches.

In a cold sauté pan add garlic and butter. Turn on high and gently swirl the ingredients in pan. The garlic will start to lightly brown in the butter. When this happens, add the kale and lightly toss until wilted.

Add water and sugar to a sauce pot. Turn on high and allow sugar to caramelize to a nice golden brown. Don't stir the sugar! Add shallot and vinegar. Cook until the caramelized sugar dissolves. Add cherries and simmer 5 minutes. Season to taste.

Slice duck and place on top of corn fritter. Drizzle with cherry gastrique and place kale on the side.

Wine Pairing:
Fusee — Syrah

Aris's Wine Notes: Duck needs a tannic red to counteract the fat. In this dish, the bing cherry gastrique provides balance for the duck's fat and brings the cherries to the forefront as another flavor. The wine I was looking for now would be rich in red fruit flavors, but with soft tannins. Fusee Syrah fit the bill. The refreshing cherry and cranberry flavors are framed with cocoa and sweet oak nuances.

Whole Wheat Linguini with Duck, Wild Mushrooms and Asiago

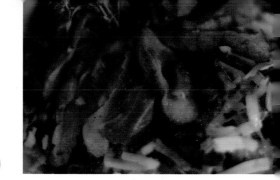

From: Mangia Mangia • 100 State Street • Columbia, SC 29169

Pan sear duck breasts in oil in a hot sauté pan. Cook 2 to 3 minutes per side for medium-rare. Let rest.

Cover mushrooms with boiling water and allow to reconstitute for 3 minutes. Remove mushrooms. Strain liquid and reserve.

Brown pancetta in a hot sauté pan. Remove from pan. Sauté garlic and leeks in pancetta fat. Add mushrooms. Deglaze mushroom pan with Madeira. Add thyme and parsley. Add ½ cup of mushroom liquid and chicken stock to sauté pan and reduce by half. Add butter and season to taste.

Cook pasta in boiling water for about 2 minutes. Remove and toss with mushroom sauce.

Place pasta in bowl. Top with sliced duck breast and sprinkle cheese on top.

Wine Pairing:
Finca Sophenia 'Altosur' Merlot

Aris's Wine Notes: This is not the soft, easy drinking Merlot of California, but the Merlot of a country that is number one in beef consumption. The tannins easily slice through the fatty, protein-rich duck. The mushrooms and Asiago add complexity to the dish that is matched by flavors of plum, cherry and black currant fruit, a peppery and sweet vanilla spice and hints of violets.

2 duck breasts, scored on fat side
2 teaspoons olive oil
2 cups dried wild mushrooms
3 cups boiling water
1 cup diced pancetta
2 tablespoons chopped garlic
1 cup leeks, sliced
1 cup Madeira wine
1 tablespoon thyme, chopped
1 tablespoon parsley, chopped
1 cup chicken stock
2 tablespoons butter
salt and pepper to taste
¼ pound fresh whole wheat linguini
   (or other pasta)
1 cup grated Asiago

Makes 4 servings

Thom's Tips: You have heard of Parmesan and Romano. What is Asiago? Asiago has been made in Italy for more than 1,000 years. It comes from the alpine region close to Switzerland. It is made from cow's milk that is exceptionally rich because the cows graze on the hearty mountain grasses.

Chicken Florentine Al' Orange with Caprese Cucumber Salad

From: Villa Romana • 707 South Kings Hwy • Myrtle Beach, SC 29577

1 cup orange juice

1 cup heavy cream

garlic powder (a pinch)

salt and pepper to taste

¼ cup dry white wine

4 (7-ounce) chicken breasts

1 cup cooked spinach, seasoned with
   salt, pepper, garlic and butter

1 baton prosciutto ham

provolone cheese, cut into sticks
   about ¼ inch thick

egg wash

flour

canola oil

1 cup thinly sliced mushrooms

1 tablespoon pine nuts

½ cup grated mozzarella

Caprese Cucumber Salad

3 Roma tomatoes, diced

1 cucumber, diced

2 ovolone, diced (fresh mozzarella)

5 to 6 fresh basil leaves, chopped

salt and pepper

extra virgin olive oil

Makes 4 servings

Thom's Tips: When wrapping chicken around various ingredients, you may need toothpicks to hold the rolls together. Remove the toothpicks before serving.

Preheat oven to 500 degrees F.

Mix orange juice, cream, garlic powder, salt, pepper and wine in a saucepan. Reduce until a medium-thick sauce consistency.

Split and pound chicken breasts. Wrap flattened chicken around spinach, prosciutto ham and provolone. Dip roll in egg wash, then in flour. Sauté in pan with oil until chicken is done. Place in baking dish and top with mushrooms, pine nuts, orange sauce and mozzarella. Put in oven for 6 minutes, or until the cheese is melted.

Place one chicken wrap on a plate. Spoon on orange sauce and mushrooms. Finish plate with cucumber salad.

Caprese Cucumber Salad: Mix all ingredients in a salad bowl and serve.

Wine Pairing:
Custoza — Lugana

Aris's Wine Notes: Italian wine with Italian food is usually safe, but why a wine from the lowly Trebbiano grape, one of the world's "Rodney Dangerfield" grapes that just "can't get no respect"? The lovely floral and citrus flavors combine with mineral notes and a hint of almond to blend nicely with the dish, while the crisp acidity cleanses the palate.

Meat

Angus Barn
Shell Steak

From: Angus Barn Restaurant • 9401 Glenwood Avenue • Raleigh, NC 27617

4 (15-ounce) bone-in New York
    strips
salt and pepper
1 Vidalia onion
2 large tomatoes, diced
1 cup pitted kalamata olives
½ cup olive oil
1 cup feta cheese
½ cup balsamic vinegar
extra virgin olive oil
1 bunch asparagus, washed and cut
    to 3 inches
1 cup sliced shiitake mushrooms
2 pre-baked potatoes
2 tablespoons Cajun seasoning

Angus Barn Steak Seasoning

1 teaspoon garlic powder
1 teaspoon oregano
1 teaspoon basil
1 teaspoon celery salt
½ teaspoon salt
1 teaspoon pepper
1 clove garlic, minced

Makes 4 servings

Start your grill.

Season steaks with salt and pepper and Angus Barn Steak Seasoning. Place on medium-hot grill, cook approximately 3 to 4 minutes on each side to medium-well. Remove from heat and allow to rest.

Peel onion and then cut onion, tomatoes and kalamata olives. Sauté with olive oil until onion is tender. Add feta cheese, vinegar, extra virgin olive oil, salt and pepper. Mix together.

Blanch asparagus. Remove from heat and then place in an ice bath.

Slice shiitake mushrooms. Sauté in olive oil, salt and pepper. Add asparagus and continue to sauté.

Cut pre-baked potatoes into quarters. Season with Cajun seasoning. Fry potatoes in oil until crispy. Remove from oil and drain on paper towels.

Place steak on plate. Top with onion mixture. Arrange mushrooms and asparagus on the side along with the potato wedges.

Angus Barn Steak Seasoning: Combine all ingredients together and set aside.

Wine Pairing:
Mondavi — Cabernet Sauvignon

Aris's Wine Notes: This dish screams for a classic Napa Cabernet. One that will do justice is a Robert Mondavi. Solid, integrated tannins and toasty vanilla oak frame layers of blackberry, cassis, mineral and black licorice character. These flavors match well with the beef, mushrooms and green herbs and the wine has adequate depth to handle the feta cheese.

Thom's Tips: Resting a steak is always a challenge for me. It's hot off the grill or out of the broiler and I just want a taste of the sizzling beauty. I know the chefs always say that you should let the steak rest for 2 to 3 minutes. This way the juices firm up and stay in the steak, instead of running all over your plate. Yes, I know: letting the steak rest will make it much juicier and taste better. But 2 to 3 minutes . . . I'm hungry now!

Filet au Poivre

From: Angus Barn Restaurant • 9401 Glenwood Avenue • Raleigh, NC 27617

4 (10-ounce) filet mignons
cracked black pepper
3 tablespoons chopped shallots
2 teaspoons chopped garlic
olive oil
½ cup red wine
¼ cup red wine vinegar
1 cup beef or veal stock
pinch of cracked black pepper
¼ cup cognac
½ cup heavy cream
salt and pepper to taste
2 pre-baked potatoes
2 teaspoons olive oil
2 teaspoons butter
1 clove garlic, chopped
½ pound fresh green beans
1 red bell pepper, julienned
salt and pepper
juice of ½ lemon

Makes 4 servings

Thom's Tips: Time to learn another cooking term. Julienne. To julienne ingredients cut them into long, thin matchstick-sized strips. When julienning food, remember to cut slowly and carefully so as to avoid creating long thin matchstick strips of your fingers.

Start your grill.

Dust filets with cracked black pepper. Grill to a perfect medium-rare, 5 to 6 minutes on each side. Allow to rest 2 to 3 minutes before serving.

Sauté shallots and garlic in olive oil. Add wine, vinegar, stock (preferably homemade, but canned is acceptable) and a pinch of cracked black pepper; simmer. Add cognac, then heavy cream. Season with salt and pepper. Leave on low heat until ready to plate dish.

Cut pre-baked potatoes into thin strips. Deep-fry until crispy and golden brown.

Heat sauté pan with equal parts of olive oil and butter. Sauté garlic and then add green beans and red pepper. Season with salt, pepper and lemon juice.

Place filet on plate. Ladle sauce over top and then place green beans and fried potatoes next to filet.

Wine Pairing:
Mondavi — Merlot

Aris's Wine Notes: I choose Mondavi's Merlot for the flavor combination of beef with the Bordeaux grapes. I choose Merlot because I need a wine with the least amount of astringent tannins so as to not clash with the strong black pepper. I choose Mondavi because I can always count on the winery to deliver the ideal wine, true to its grape variety and its region.

Meat Loaf Stuffed with Blue Cheese, Tomato and Bacon

From: Fenwick's On Providence • 511 Providence Road • Charlotte, NC 28207

Preheat oven to 350 degrees F.

Mix the meat loaf ingredients in a large mixing bowl. (It is best to use your hands to mix all of the ingredients together.) Add breadcrumbs so that the meat loaf holds together. It should have the consistency of soft Play-Doh.

Line a baking sheet with a generous amount of foil. Spray the foil thoroughly with non-stick spray. Pat out the meat loaf so that it completely covers the baking sheet evenly.

Lay the tomato slices along the center of the meat loaf. Top with blue cheese and bacon. Use the foil to help fold the edges to the middle, shaping tightly into a loaf. Make sure the loaf is smooth and sealed. Bend the foil over the loaf and seal completely.

Bake for about 1 hour. Unfold foil and bake 15 minutes more. At this point, if you like, brush ketchup or BBQ sauce on top of the loaf. Remove from oven and cool. (You can even prepare this the day before.) Slice when cool and serve with mashed potatoes and a green vegetable.

Wine Pairing:

Chase — Centennial Harvest Zinfandel

Aris's Wine Notes: The fruitiness billows out of the glass and consumes the palate with a multi-dimensional array of flavors reminiscent of blueberries, raspberries and mocha spiced with cinnamon, vanilla and cedar. This Zinfandel is what we need to tackle the blue cheese and bacon stuffing.

Meat Loaf

2 pounds ground beef

1 cup breadcrumbs

½ cup finely chopped onion

½ cup finely chopped celery

⅓ cup milk

2 eggs, beaten

⅓ cup ketchup

2 teaspoons salt

1 teaspoon black pepper

1 teaspoon dried oregano

Filling

2 tomatoes, sliced

1 to 2 cups blue cheese

9 slices cooked bacon, crumbled

Makes 6 to 8 servings

Thom's Tips: Dried herbs are perfect for sauces. Because they are dried, the herbs actually absorb the moisture of the sauce that they are in while releasing their oils. Because the herbs are dried, their tasty oils are concentrated and more powerful.

Balsamic-Braised Short Ribs with Pan Sauce over Roasted Garlic Mashed Potatoes

From: Solstice Kitchen and Wine Bar • 841-4 Sparkleberry Lane • Columbia, SC 29229

4 (1-pound) beef short ribs
(1½ to 2 inches thick)
salt and pepper
olive oil
3 cloves garlic, smashed
1 cup chopped onion
½ cup chopped celery
½ cup chopped carrots
1 cup red wine
1 cup balsamic vinegar
1 cup beef broth
3 tablespoons rosemary
2 tablespoons thyme
4 large potatoes, peeled and diced
1 clove garlic
½ cup milk
2 teaspoons roasted garlic
2 tablespoons butter
½ pound fresh green beans
1 red bell pepper, sliced
1 tablespoon olive oil

Makes 4 to 6 servings

Thom's Tips: Just about all of the recipes in this cookbook can be created in 30 minutes or less. This recipe takes 4 hours. There is just no way to cook ribs fast. The meat starts off tough. The low heat of 325 degrees F for 3½ hours makes the meat "fall off the bone" tender. I've tried to cook ribs faster, but it's just not the same.

Preheat oven to 325 degrees F.

Season ribs with salt and pepper. Brown with olive oil in a sauté pan on both sides. Remove from pan and place in a roasting pan and set aside.

Sweat garlic, onion and celery in a medium saucepan with olive oil. Add carrots. Deglaze with wine. Add vinegar, broth, rosemary and thyme. Pour sauce over short ribs and put in oven. Bake for 3 to 3 ½ hours. Remove ribs from pan. Pour braising sauce into saucepan and reduce liquid into a sauce.

Place potatoes in boiling water with salt and garlic. Cook until the potatoes are tender. Remove from stove, then drain and mash potatoes. Add hot milk, garlic, salt, pepper and butter. Mix and mash all ingredients and set aside.

Blanch green beans in boiling water. Remove from water and drop into ice bath. Sauté green beans with red peppers, olive oil and salt and pepper.

Place mashed potatoes on plate. Top with a couple of short ribs. Drizzle braising sauce over ribs and potatoes. Place vegetables on side.

Wine Pairing:
Domaine Serene — Evenstad Reserve Pinot Noir

Aris's Wine Notes: If America had an appellation system similar to France, then Domaine Serene would be classed a First Growth and the Evenstad Vineyard would be a Grand Cru. This Pinot Noir has the classic "steel fist in a velvet glove" impact on the palate. It's like a bowling ball, dense yet perfectly round and polished. It's hard to imagine a dish that would not be enhanced by this wine. In fact, the wine is so rich, complex and complete, it's almost a meal in itself.

Filet Mignon
Egg Rolls

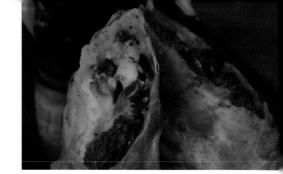

From: The Plantation Room at Celebration Hotel • 700 Bloom Street • Celebration, FL 34747

1½ pounds filet mignon pieces

3 tablespoons star anise

salt and pepper

3 tablespoons garlic

1 tablespoon ginger

1 tablespoon lemongrass

½ jalapeño

2 tablespoons sesame oil

6 egg roll wrappers

1 egg, beaten

2 tablespoons water

10 ounces Boursin cheese

2 quarts canola oil, for frying

sweet chili sauce

Make 6 servings

Thom's Tips: Experiment. Try new combinations with main ingredients. Remember: have no fear. When things don't work, it is still usually edible. But when they do, it is amazing. The worst-case scenario is that you have to throw stuff away and order a pizza. But the best-case scenario is that people are stunned, speechless, awed by what you have made.

Clean most of the fat from the filet. Dice it small. Grind star anise in a spice grinder or coffee grinder until fine. Season beef with salt, pepper and star anise. Chop garlic, ginger, lemongrass and jalapeño into small pieces. Mix together with beef. In a large sauté pan, cook beef in sesame oil until medium-rare. Remove from heat and let cool 5 minutes.

Egg wash the egg roll wrappers with a mixture of the egg and water.

Place about ⅓ cup of beef and 3 tablespoons cheese onto your wrapper. Roll in wrapper. Make sure the ends are sealed. Deep fry the egg rolls for 4 minutes.

Serve with sweet chili sauce.

Wine Pairing:
Ferrari-Carano — Merlot

Aris's Wine Notes: This is what Merlot ought to be, ripe, juicy and lush but not wimpy. The Merlot grapes deliver dark berry flavors of cherry and currants that are a classic match for beef. The rich fruit of the Merlot complements the spices, while its soft texture is contrasted by the crunchy wrap.

Black Angus Aged Beef Tenderloin with Crabmeat

From: Inn at Brevard • 410 East Main Street • Brevard, NC 28712

Start your grill.

Mix together marinade ingredients. Soak beef in marinade for 24 hours before grilling. Have grill very hot and grill beef to desired temperature.

Inn at Brevard Béarnaise Sauce:

Bring to a boil in a sauté pan, the dried tarragon and 4 tablespoons of vinegar. Let sit for 5 minutes and then drain.

Combine in blender, remaining vinegar, yolks, garlic, butter and Tabasco. Keep the blender at full speed until the mixture is thick and creamy. Taste often and add salt, pepper and more butter, if needed. Add French tarragon mixture at this point. Refrigerate total mixture and serve cold or at room temperature. Never heat the béarnaise sauce.

Serve beef with lump crabmeat, then drizzle with béarnaise sauce.

Wine Pairing:

Leaping Lizard — Pinot Noir

Aris's Wine Notes: Pinot Noir is my favorite solution to the "red wine with fish" problem, but I needed one with enough richness to handle the beef and sauce without the tannins usually associated with robust reds. My search lead me to California and the Leaping Lizard winery. Their Pinot Noir fit all the requirements.

4 (8-ounce) beef tenderloin filets
1 cup lump crabmeat

Marinade
½ cup extra virgin olive oil
½ cup aged balsamic vinegar
½ cup chopped fresh garlic
½ cup chopped Vidalia onion
⅓ cup Worcestershire sauce
salt and pepper to taste

Inn at Brevard Béarnaise Sauce
2 tablespoons dried French tarragon
6 tablespoons white distilled or tarragon vinegar, divided
6 egg yolks
1 tablespoon chopped fresh garlic
10 tablespoons melted butter (hot)
1 tablespoon Tabasco

Makes 4 servings

Thom's Tips: Finish the beef off in the oven. Sear the meat and deglaze the pan. Put the meat in a 350-degree oven. Then finish your sides. That way, all of the elements of your meal are finished at the same time and can be served hot.

Beef Tenderloin Carpetbagger with Fried Oysters, Sweet Soy and Chili Oil

From: Bovine's Wood Fired Grill • 3979 Hwy 17 Business • Murrells Inlet, SC 29576

24 large fresh oysters, shucked

1 (5.2-ounce) Boursin cheese

¼ cup breadcrumbs, panko preferred

4 (8-ounce) beef tenderloin filets

salt and pepper

1 cup Cabernet or other rich red wine

1 cup veal stock

1 pound Yukon potatoes, peeled

4 tablespoons butter

1 tablespoon rosemary

1 pint heavy cream

2 cups peanut oil

¼ cup flour

2 eggs, beaten

1 cup panko breadcrumbs

1 bottle sweet soy sauce

1 bottle chili oil

Makes 4 servings

Thom's Tips: Never quite sure when boiled potatoes are done? Stick them with your fork or knife and make sure that it goes through easily. Or just squish them and make sure that they are nice and crumbly.

Start your grill.

To make filling, mix 12 oysters, Boursin cheese and ¼ cup panko breadcrumbs. Cut a slit in each filet and make a pocket, using a knife and fingers. Stuff oyster mixture into filets. Season steaks with salt and pepper. Grill for 3 to 5 minutes on both sides, depending on desired doneness. Remove to clean plate and keep warm.

In a saucepan, combine wine and veal stock. Simmer slowly, reducing by two-thirds until sauce coats the back of a spoon. Set aside.

Boil potatoes until completely cooked. While they are cooking, heat butter, rosemary and cream in a saucepan, simmering for 20 minutes. Drain potatoes well. Combine with cream reduction. Whip with hand mixer. Season with salt and pepper to taste. Set aside in a warm place.

Heat peanut oil in a deep sauté pan. Dredge remaining oysters in flour, then egg, then panko. Fry to golden brown and remove from oil. Drain well.

To plate, divide potatoes evenly among four plates, placing in center. Place filet on top. Place three fried oysters on each plate around filet. Ladle veal wine reduction over and around. Drizzle oysters with sweet soy and chili oil.

Wine Pairing:

Ravenswood — Dickerson Vineyard Zinfandel

Aris's Wine Notes: This bold and complex dish really needs a powerful wine for the marriage to work, and who do I turn to when power is the name of the game? Ravenswood, of course, where "no wimpy wines" is the motto. This Dickerson Vineyard Zinfandel combines complexity and balance to give a complete package.

Pan-Seared Filet Mignon
with Roasted Garlic, Gorgonzola and Balsamic Butter

From: Mangia Mangia • 100 State Street • Columbia, SC 29169

1 bulb garlic, whole and unpeeled

¼ cup extra virgin olive oil

2 tablespoons vegetable oil

4 steaks of your choice

salt and pepper

1 cup Gorgonzola cheese, at room temperature

1 cup aged balsamic vinegar

1 stick butter

2 bulbs fennel, julienned

1 pound arugula, washed

Makes 4 servings

Thom's Tips: When cooking meat, resist the temptation of taking it out of the refrigerator and putting it immediately over the heat. Instead, let it warm to room temperature before you begin cooking. This allows the meat to cook faster and more evenly.

Preheat oven to 450 degrees F.

Slice the top off of the garlic bulb. Place in a roasting pan cut side down with olive oil. Roast in oven for 15 to 20 minutes, until garlic bulb is soft. Remove from oven. Drain garlic oil and mix with vegetable oil, reserving garlic bulb.

Season steaks with salt and pepper and then set aside.

Heat mixed oils in a sauté pan. When slightly smoking, add steaks. Sear to desired temperature, 3 to 4 minutes each side for medium-rare, depending on cut and size of steak.

Squeeze garlic from bulb. Roughly chop garlic, then mix with Gorgonzola.

Reduce vinegar by two-thirds in a saucepan. Remove from heat and whisk in butter.

Sauté fennel in olive oil over medium heat until soft. Turn up heat, add arugula and toss until slightly wilted.

Serve steaks on bed of fennel and arugula topped with garlic and cheese mixture. Drizzle with balsamic butter.

Wine Pairing:
Ruffino — Chianti Classico Riserva Ducale Oro

Aris's Wine Notes: If you needed a Chianti to use as a benchmark, this is it. The nose is floral and fruity. The rich Sangiovese fruit has exceptional depth and length. It has an elegance, harmony and restrained power reminiscent of the finest Bordeaux. Then, just when you think it can't get better, along comes a dish like this and the gastronomic fireworks begin.

Mike Wallace's Filet and Crab Napoleon

From: Red Rocks Café • **4223-8 Providence Road** • **Charlotte, NC 28211**

Put potatoes in a saucepan with cold water. Bring to a boil and cook until potatoes are soft.

In a hot sauté pan with oil, sear filet medallions on each side until medium-rare. Remove medallions from pan. Add crabmeat to pan and cook until lightly browned. Remove crab from pan and set aside. Deglaze pan with port and then reduce. Add demi-glace to pan and reduce until sauce.

Blanch asparagus in boiling water. Sauté blanched asparagus in oil, garlic, salt and pepper.

Strain potatoes. Mix potatoes with hand mixer. Add butter, garlic, cream, salt and pepper.

Ladle sauce onto plate. Spoon potatoes into center of dish. Wrap asparagus around potatoes. Place one filet medallion on potatoes. Spoon half the cooked crab on top of medallion. Place second filet on crab and medallion. Spoon the rest of the crab onto medallion. Place third filet on medallion and crab tower. Top with alfalfa sprouts.

Wine Pairing:
Robert Mondavi — Cabernet Sauvignon 'Private Selection'

Aris's Wine Notes: Winemaking talent is more often expressed in the ability to make a good inexpensive wine than the ability to make a great expensive wine. The Robert Mondavi winery has a proven ability to make those great expensive wines, but with this wine they show that a fine, classically-flavored Cabernet can be made with consistency at an easily affordable price for everyday enjoyment. Ripe plums and blackberry flavors laced with vanilla spiced oak and finished with soft tannins make this a fine choice for this dish.

3 potatoes, peeled and diced
2 tablespoons oil
12 (3-ounce) filet medallions
1 pound lump crabmeat
1 cup port
1 cup demi-glace
12 stalks asparagus
extra virgin olive oil
2 tablespoons roasted garlic
salt and pepper to taste
3 tablespoons butter, unsalted
2 cloves garlic, minced
1 cup heavy cream
¼ cup alfalfa sprouts

Makes 4 servings

Thom's Tips: If you're making mashed potatoes, make sure your milk is warm when you add it to the potatoes. Cold milk will cause the starches to retract, keeping the potatoes from becoming as creamy as they can be.

Curried Noodles
with Flank Steak

From: Jujube Restaurant—Asian Kitchen and Bar • **1201-L Raleigh Road** • **Chapel Hill, NC 27514**

3 tablespoons fish sauce

1½ tablespoons chili oil

1½ tablespoons sweet chili sauce

3 tablespoons brown sugar

½ stalk lemongrass, finely chopped

2 pounds flank steak, trimmed

½ onion, finely diced

2 tablespoons yellow curry paste

1 (8-ounce) can coconut milk

salt and sugar

1 (8-ounce) package medium
    Chinese wheat noodles

1 cup bok choy, blanched and
    chopped

2 cups spinach, blanched

1 cup julienned carrots, blanched

Makes 4 servings

Thom's Tips: You can make some of the toughest and cheapest cuts of meat soft and tender with the help of a marinade. Flank steak is a classic example. The longer you marinate it, the more tender it becomes. The marinade actually breaks down the fibers in the steak. For the best results marinate the steak for up to 2 days in your refrigerator.

Start your grill.

Combine fish sauce, chili oil, chili sauce, sugar and lemongrass in a large container. Add flank steak and coat. Marinate overnight or for at least 1 hour. Grill to medium-rare. Allow to rest at room temp for 5 minutes and slice against grain.

Process the onion and curry paste together in a food processor until smooth. Pour in pan and sauté the mix for a few minutes. Add coconut milk and bring to a simmer. Add salt and sugar as needed. Set aside.

Cook noodles in boiling salted water until al dente. Drain and toss with bok choy, spinach and julienned carrots. Distribute to bowls and ladle hot yellow curry sauce over top. Top with warm steak.

Wine Pairing:
Swings & Roundabouts — Cabernet Sauvignon

Aris's Wine Notes: The Aussies love to give cute names to their wines, but make no mistake: this is a serious Cabernet that is rich, complex and exquisitely balanced. For the sweet and spicy curry, I wanted a wine of depth and richness with a structure that was firm but not astringent.

Grilled Filet
with Grilled Gorgonzola Polenta

From: La Cave Restaurant • **329 South Church Street** • **Salisbury, NC 28144**

Preheat the grill.

Preheat oven to 350 degrees F.

In a pot or pan, heat brown sauce, wine, bay leaves, shallot and peppercorns, and reduce by half to make a demi-glace.

In a different pot, bring the stock to a boil. Whisk in the polenta and reduce heat to medium or low. Stir constantly for about 3 minutes until you have a creamy consistency (not too dry or too loose). Add Gorgonzola, Parmesan and butter and season to taste. Spread the polenta on a baking pan lined with wax paper. Let cool (this can be done the day before). Cut the polenta into medallions about 3 inches in diameter and ½ inch thick.

Season filets with salt and pepper. Spread or spray butter or oil on the grill. Grill filets to desired temperature.

Cut the red onion into ½-inch medallions. Season with salt and pepper. Spread or spray onion with oil. Grill about 3 to 4 minutes. Spread or spray polenta with oil. Bake polenta until golden brown, about 3 to 4 minutes.

Place the polenta in the middle of the plate. Stack the red onion on top of the polenta. Place the filet on top of the onion and then pour demi-glace on top of the filet.

Wine Pairing:
Frei Brothers —— Cabernet Sauvignon

Aris's Wine Notes: Although the filet is a delicate-flavored cut, the Gorgonzola kicks it up a notch or two, requiring a richly textured wine as well as one with complementary flavors. The lush texture gives the wine a sun-ripened sweetness that balances the saltiness of the cheese.

2 cups brown sauce

2 cups red wine

2 bay leaves

1 shallot, chopped

6 peppercorns

2 cups chicken stock

1 cup polenta

4 tablespoons Gorgonzola

4 tablespoons grated Parmesan

½ stick butter

4 (10-ounce) filets, trimmed

salt and pepper

1 red onion

Makes 4 servings

Thom's Tips: When cooking filet mignon, cook the meat on all 6 faces. Yup, 6 faces: top, bottom, and all 4 sides. In filet mignon cuts, the meat resembles a cube. Searing the meat on all sides keeps all of those important juices locked inside the steak. If you have seared the meat on all sides and it is till too rare for your taste, just put it in the oven at 350 degrees to cook the inside without charring the outside of the meat.

Pecan-Crusted Flatiron Steak with Green Chilaquiles and Black Bean Coulis

From: The Prickly Pear • 761 North Main Street • Mooresville, NC 28115

2 (8-ounce) flat iron steaks

¼ cup pecan meal

2 to 3 tablespoons olive oil

1 to 2 medium tomatoes, roasted or grilled

1 cup black beans

½ cup water

3 toasted chiles de arbol

1 tablespoon balsamic vinegar

½ teaspoon Mexican oregano

2 cloves roasted garlic

salt

3 ears corn (grilled and kernels removed from ears)

2 cloves garlic

¼ cup cider vinegar

juice of ½ lime

fresh ground black pepper

2 cups canola oil

½ teaspoon chopped onion

1 tablespoon chopped mushrooms

2 tablespoons canola oil

12 corn tortillas (fried and broken into pieces)

queso blanco or grated Monterey jack cheese

2 tablespoons heavy cream

1 tablespoon crema fresca or sour cream

¼ cup Tomatillo Sauce (see next page)

Preheat oven to 400 degrees F.

Bread steaks with pecan meal. Preheat searing pan to medium-high. Sear steaks in olive oil on one side and then flip. Remove from stove top and place in oven until steak is cooked to desired temperature.

Bring tomatoes, black beans and water to a boil and reduce heat to low. Place in a blender and purée with chiles, vinegar, oregano and garlic. Add salt to taste, then strain.

Combine corn, garlic, vinegar, lime juice and pepper in a blender and purée. Strain ingredients. Add liquid back to blender. While the blender is on, slowly drizzle in 2 cups canola oil to create emulsion.

Sauté onion and mushroom in pan with 2 tablespoons canola oil over medium heat. Add tortilla chips, cheese, heavy cream, crema fresca and Tomatillo Sauce; toss ingredients thoroughly in pan. Cook until sauce sticks to the chips and thickens.

Ladle beans onto plate. Slice steaks and place on the beans. Pour cheese sauce over steak. Add extra Tomatillo Sauce, if desired.

Tomatillo Sauce: Combine canola oil, tomatillos, jalapeños, onion and garlic in large saucepan over medium heat. Fry for approximately 15 minutes, being careful not to overcook tomatillos. Remove from stove and pour into blender to purée contents. Add cumin and salt to taste.

Wine Pairing:
Blackstone — Cabernet Sauvignon

Aris's Wine Notes: While there are enough tannins for structure, the focus here is on the dark berry and plum fruit and toasty oak, with hints of licorice. While classic Cabernet flavors pair well with steak, Mexican dishes require wines with a rich but soft texture to balance their spice and heat. That's where this Blackstone shines.

Tomatillo Sauce

2 cups canola oil
10 tomatillos
2 jalapeños
¼ yellow onion, chopped
2 cloves garlic
1 tablespoon ground cumin
½ teaspoon salt

Makes 4 servings

Thom's Tips: Every time you flip a steak you allow the juices to run out. If you flip it over and over again, you'll end up with a steak that's the consistency of beef jerky. Resist, hold back, refrain, stand firm and defy the urge to flip more than once. You can do it.

Vanilla Beef Fajitas

From: Salsa Mexican Caribbean Restaurant • 6 Patton Avenue • Asheville, NC 28801

3 chipotle peppers, chopped

2 cloves garlic, chopped

¼ cup olive oil

½ tablespoon pepper

½ tablespoon salt

1 tablespoon vanilla

1 pound skirt steak, trimmed and
cut into large pieces

Avocado and Caper Salsa

½ fire-roasted bell pepper, diced

1 avocado, diced

1 tomato, diced

1 red onion, diced

2 cloves garlic, diced

¼ cup capers

¼ cup light olive oil

juice from ½ lime

¼ cup chopped fresh cilantro

Coconut and Annatto Seed Sauce

1 tablespoon masa flour

1 stick butter

½ (15-ounce) can coconut milk

2 tablespoons coconut oil

¼ tablespoon rosemary

1 tablespoon annatto powder

4 dry ancho chiles

½ tablespoon salt

Makes 4 to 6 servings

Start your grill.

Mix together chipotle peppers, garlic, olive oil, pepper, salt and vanilla. Place beef in mixture. Marinate a couple of hours, preferably overnight.

Remove beef from marinade. Pan sear or grill beef 5 minutes per side.

Slice and serve with Avocado and Caper Salsa and Coconut and Annatto Seed Sauce.

Avocado and Caper Salsa:

Grill bell pepper over flame or broil in oven, turning the pepper until the skin all the way around is slightly burnt and pulling from the pepper. Remove from heat. Place in a paper bag to cool. Once cool, remove burnt skin. Dice avocado, red pepper, tomato, onion and cloves. Mix with capers, olive oil, lime juice and cilantro. Set aside.

Coconut and Annatto Seed Sauce:

In a sauté pan, add flour and butter. Cook for 3 minutes over high heat. Slowly add coconut milk, coconut oil, rosemary, annatto powder, anchos and salt. Heat the ingredients. Remove from heat. Set aside.

Wine Pairing:
Liberty School — Cabernet Sauvignon

Aris's Wine Notes: Beef with Cabernet is a no brainer, right? Well, sort of, but with all the spicy flavors going on in this dish, we need to be a little careful. Cabernet Sauvignon takes on a unique personality with each distinctive climate it encounters. Liberty School Cabernet emphasizes the fruit-driven power necessary to handle the spices. The wine will not fight with the spicy heat, but will balance it with its juicy, ripe fruit.

Thom's Tips: One of the fastest and most fun ways of unwrapping and crushing garlic is . . . brute force. Take a garlic clove and lay it on the cutting board. Place the flat side of your chef's knife on top of the garlic clove. While hanging onto the chef's knife with one hand, make a fist with the other hand. Hit the flat part of the blade that is directly over the garlic clove, smashing it to oblivion. Remove the skin and dice or chop, if required.

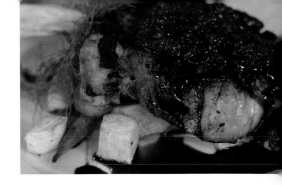

Veal Chop

From: 45 South • 20 East Broad Street • Savannah, GA 31401

1 cup balsamic vinegar

1 red bell pepper, de-stemmed and chopped roughly

½ onion, peeled and chopped roughly

1 pint cherry tomatoes, halved

2 cloves garlic, peeled

1 tablespoon fennel seed

½ cup Dijon mustard

4 (6- to 8-ounce) veal chops

½ bulb fennel, cored and cubed

4 baby carrots with tops, peeled

2 turnips, peeled and cubed

8 fingerling potatoes, sliced 1 inch thick

3 tablespoons olive oil

salt and pepper to taste

½ cup basil, leaves only

½ cup mint, leaves only

½ bulb roasted garlic

2 tablespoons pine nuts

3 tablespoons olive oil

Makes 4 servings

Thom's Tips: A tip I learned from Aris. If you open more than one bottle of wine at a time, store them in the refrigerator; this includes reds. But remember to take the reds out an hour before serving. Reds taste best at 65–68 degrees.

Preheat oven to 350 degrees F.

Blend together vinegar, bell pepper, onion, tomatoes and garlic. Add fennel seed once other ingredients are fully processed. Fold in Dijon. Dip veal chops into this marinade. Let sit 10 to 15 minutes. Grill 5 to 7 minutes per side for medium-rare.

Coat vegetables in olive oil. Season with salt and pepper. Roast in oven until tender.

Blend basil, mint, garlic and pine nuts in food processor. Drizzle in olive oil. Add salt and pepper to taste.

Place vegetables on plate. Top with veal chop. Drizzle dish with basil/mint sauce.

Wine Pairing:
Ravenswood — Belloni Vineyard Zinfandel

Aris's Wine Notes: A big chunk of veal, marinated in balsamic vinaigrette and smothered in herbs just screams for Zinfandel. So, where do you go when you need a Zin? Well, to the Zin masters of course, Ravenswood. Their mantra is "no wimpy wines" and boy do they deliver on that. A match made in heaven, but to be enjoyed in the here and now.

Veal Rib Chop
au Poivre

From: Vinnie's Steakhouse & Seafood • 7440 Six Forks Road • Raleigh, NC 27615

Crush peppercorns until well cracked by using the underside of the sauté pan. Rub both sides of veal chops with cracked peppercorns. Grill chops with a little butter.

In a sauté pan, sear remaining peppercorns in butter. Caution: this next step can be dangerous. Stand back and add brandy. Flambé peppercorns in brandy. When flame subsides, add heavy cream and reduce. Add salt to taste.

Sauté mushrooms in oil, salt and pepper. Add wine and reduce. Add to cream mix.

Top veal chop with mushroom and pepper sauce. Garnish with parsley.

Wine Pairing:

Ravenswood — 'Icon' Syrah

Aris's Wine Notes: A rich, succulent chunk of meat, an opulent and mouth-coating creamy sauce and spicy peppercorns. What wine can we pair with this dish? How about a chunky, meaty, opulent, creamy-textured wine with a peppery spiciness. It comes from my favorite "no wimpy wines" winery, Ravenswood, and they call this big black beauty "Icon." What flavors can you expect? Try an amalgam of black fruits with notes of smoke and leather. Enough talk, lets eat and drink!

6 tablespoons peppercorns
4 (10- to 12-ounce) veal rib chops
8 tablespoons butter
½ cup brandy
1 cup heavy cream
salt
1 cup sliced mushrooms
olive oil
salt and pepper
¼ cup red wine
fresh Italian parsley

Makes 4 servings

Thom's Tips: An easy way to roughly crack peppercorns. Don't want to spend all day crushing peppercorns with a pepper mill. Sprinkle peppercorns onto a baking pan. Take your sauté pan and roll it over the peppercorns, breaking the peppercorns into rough chunks.

Seared Veal Cutlets with
Pan-Roasted Lobster and Potato Hash

From: The Speedway Club • Lowe's Motor Speedway • PO Box 600 • Concord, NC 28027

4 (3½-ounce) veal cutlets

salt and pepper

4 tablespoons clarified butter

1 ear fresh corn

½ cup diced red potatoes

1 cup oyster mushrooms

2 teaspoons minced garlic

2 teaspoons minced shallots

⅛ cup Madeira

½ cup veal stock

1 tablespoon rosemary, blanched
    and chopped

1 tablespoon butter

2 lobster tails (split lengthwise)

½ cup white wine

Makes 4 servings

Thom's Tips: Clarified butter is regular ole butter that has been melted and separated from the butter solids. This leaves what looks like a yellow oil. Clarified butter has several great properties. It does not solidify as easily as regular butter, thus it's great for dipping your seafood in. Plus, it burns at a much higher temperature than regular butter, making it better for searing meats.

Preheat oven to 350 degrees F.

Season veal with salt and pepper and sear over medium-high heat in the clarified butter until golden brown on one side. Turn over and repeat. Remove from stove top. Place in oven and cook until medium-rare, about 5 to 7 minutes.

While veal is roasting, cut corn from cob. Sauté corn in a hot pan to achieve a little color. Add the potatoes and oyster mushrooms and lightly brown. Add the garlic and shallots and sweat (careful not to burn). Deglaze the pan with the Madeira and reduce to dry. Add the stock and reduce by two-thirds. Stir in the chopped rosemary. Remove from heat and stir in the butter, being careful not to bring to a boil. Season with salt and pepper.

When veal is finished, place on a plate and let rest while cooking the lobster tail. In the same hot pan as the veal, sear the lobster, cut side down. When lightly browned, turn over and sear on the shell side. Deglaze the pan with the white wine.

Place the mushrooms and corn hash in the centers of the plates with a little of the sauce running out. Layer the cutlets on top of the mushroom mixture, with the lobster tail on top of the veal.

Wine Pairing:
Perrin — Chateauneuf du Pape 'Les Sinards'

Aris's Wine Notes: 'Les Sinards' wine has wide ranging and complex flavors and has just the right depth and complexity for the dish without overwhelming it. The flavors are a unique array of black fruits, kirsch liquor and loam, all spiced with thyme, rosemary and lavender. Richly textured with supple tannins and a long finish. This is a very harmonious and complete wine with a natural, earthy taste that is very seductive.

Veal Saltimbocca alla Romana with Fettuccine al Pesto Genovese

From: Villa Romana • **707 South Kings Hwy** • **Myrtle Beach, SC 29577**

Pound the cutlet thin (use plastic wrap). Place the prosciutto ham on one side of the cutlet. Dust the non-ham side in flour. Add 2 pieces of sage to the prosciutto side. Add butter to a non-stick frying pan. Start cooking with prosciutto side down. Almost immediately, add mushrooms and wine. Turn over the cutlets. Add 3 slices of mozzarella per cutlet. Let melt and remove from heat.

Process all Pesto Sauce ingredients in a blender until smooth.

Cook noodles according to package instructions in a pot with salted water. After noodles are done, strain. Add pesto to the cooked noodles and plate with cutlets.

Wine Pairing:
Casabianca — Chianti Colli Senesi Riserva

Aris's Wine Notes: Fully deserving of its 'Riserva' status. The structure is firm enough to handle most dishes, adding versatility to its charms. I love the way the earthy/tobacco notes blend with the mushrooms and prosciutto to create new flavors while the bright fruit cleanses the palate.

4 (3-ounce) veal cutlets
4 pieces prosciutto ham
flour
8 fresh sage leaves
2 tablespoons unsalted butter
6 mushrooms, sliced thin
1 cup white wine
2 balls fresh mozzarella, sliced into sixths
¼ pound fettuccine pasta

Pesto Sauce

6 to 12 fresh basil leaves
¾ tablespoon pine nuts
1 ½ tablespoons grated Parmesan cheese
1 clove garlic
⅓ cup extra virgin olive oil
salt and pepper

Makes 4 servings

Thom's Tips: Adding salt to your pasta water will cause it to boil faster. Salty water requires less energy to boil, so your pasta will cook faster at a higher temperature. Salt will also add flavor to your pasta.

Mustard-Encrusted
Rack of Lamb

From: City Tavern Hearst Tower • **215 South Tryon, Suite D** • **Charlotte, NC 28202**

4 (12- to 14-ounce) racks of lamb

olive oil

salt and pepper

4 tablespoons grain mustard

1 cup breadcrumbs

7 to 9 fingerling potatoes

1 tablespoon olive oil

garlic salt

cracked black pepper

1 tablespoon chopped rosemary

6 cremini mushrooms, quartered

1 teaspoon chopped garlic

2 cups arugula

½ cup sugar

1 cup dried cranberries

½ cup red wine

½ cup marmalade

rosemary sprig

Makes 4 servings

Thom's Tips: Respect the blade. Keep knives sharp and clean. Keep your fingers curled back at all times. Talk or chop, not both. Price doesn't equate to the quality of the knife. The chefs have used everything from Henckel knives that cost $180 to IKEA knives that cost $9.99. Do avoid the Ginshu type knives with the serrated edge. Sure, they can cut through a hammer, but not much else.

Preheat oven to 400 degrees F.

Sear racks of lamb in a preheated pan with olive oil. Season both sides with salt and pepper. Brush with mustard. Coat flesh side with breadcrumbs. Finish in oven 10 to 12 minutes. (Internal temperature should be 118 to 125 degrees.)

Cut fingerling potatoes in half lengthwise. Toss with olive oil, garlic salt, pepper and rosemary. Bake in oven for 20 minutes.

Sauté mushrooms and garlic. Add arugula and wilt. Season with salt and pepper.

Boil sugar with cranberries and reduce. Add wine and reduce. Add marmalade.

Cut lamb racks in half, splitting 4 bones each. Place on plates with potatoes, mushrooms and arugula. Spoon on compote. Garnish with rosemary sprig.

Wine Pairing:
Esser — Pinot Noir

Aris's Wine Notes: Rack of lamb requires a wine of richness, complexity and finesse. You want the lamb and wine to be partners, acting together in harmony with one purpose in mind—your pleasure. Pinot Noir is just the grape for the task and Esser is just the winery to provide it.

Coriander-Crusted Lamb Chops with Chimichurri

From: Gervais and Vine • 620-A Gervais Street • Columbia, SC 29201

½ cup chopped fresh cilantro
2 tablespoons ground coriander
salt and pepper
2 racks of lamb, cut into chops
olive oil

Chimichurri

1 cup loosely packed fresh mint
1 cup cilantro leaves
1 cup parsley leaves
½ medium onion, coarsely chopped
6 cloves garlic
1 teaspoon red pepper flakes
juice of 2 limes
2 tablespoons red wine vinegar
salt and pepper

Red Sangria

½ cup sugar
¼ cup water
1 large lemon
1 large orange
1 small apple, cored and thinly
   sliced
1 bottle dry red wine (Tempranillo,
   fruity Cabernet or Merlot)
½ cup Grand Marnier

Makes 4 servings

Combine cilantro and coriander. Mix well. Salt and pepper lamb chops. Coat in coriander and cilantro mix. Sauté in olive oil in hot pan.

Chimichurri:

Combine mint, cilantro, parsley, onion, garlic, red pepper flakes, lime juice and vinegar in a food processor. Process until semi-smooth, then season with salt and pepper.

Serve lamb chops with Chimichurri sauce.

Red Sangria:

Combine sugar and water in a small saucepan. Over medium heat, cook until sugar dissolves (this is simple syrup). Remove from heat and allow to cool. Thinly slice half of the lemon and half of the orange. Combine in large pitcher. Juice the other halves of the lemon and orange and add juice and rinds to the pitcher. Add the apple, wine and Grand Marnier. Add the simple syrup. Stir until well mixed. Refrigerate until thoroughly chilled, about 2 hours, or allow to macerate in the fridge overnight. Strain the old fruit. Dice up some new fruit to add to the glasses. Serve straight up or on the rocks.

Pinchitos Morunos
– Moorish Kebabs

From: Gervais and Vine • 620-A Gervais Street • Columbia, SC 29201

Combine all of the ingredients except pomegranate juice in a mixing bowl. Dump into a zip-lock bag and marinate for at least 2 hours. Thread meat onto skewers. Spray with non-stick spray and grill.

Simmer pomegranate juice approximately 30 minutes until reduced to syrupy consistency, about ¼ cup.

Raita:

Put yogurt in a strainer. Allow to drain overnight to thicken. Combine with cucumber, onion, mint, garam masala, salt and pepper.

Plate kebabs. Drizzle pomegranate syrup over kebabs. Place raita in a bowl for dipping.

Rosé Sangria:

Combine sugar and water in a small saucepan. Over medium heat, cook until sugar dissolves (this is simple syrup). Remove from heat and allow to cool. Combine all ingredients in a pitcher. Stir to mix. Refrigerate at least 8 hours or up to 48 hours. Serve over ice.

1½ pounds pork loin, chicken breast, lamb leg meat, tuna, etc., cut into ½-inch chunks
3 tablespoons olive oil
2 cloves garlic, chopped
2 medium onions, thinly sliced
½ cup chopped flat-leaf parsley
1 tablespoon ground cumin
1 tablespoon chili powder
1 teaspoon ground black pepper
1 tablespoon kosher or sea salt
2 cups pomegranate juice

Raita

2 cups plain yogurt
½ cup finely diced cucumber (peeled)
2 tablespoons finely diced red onion
2 tablespoons minced fresh mint
2 teaspoons garam masala
salt and pepper

Rosé Sangria

½ cup sugar
½ cup water
1 bottle dry Rosé wine
½ cup Grand Marnier
1 cup sliced fresh strawberries
1 cup fresh or frozen raspberries

Makes 4 servings

Pork and Beans
with Chow-Chow
and Mustard Green Salad

From: Mimosa Grill • **327 South Tryon Street** • **Charlotte, NC 28202**

olive oil or peanut oil

4 strips bacon

4 ounces fatback

2 yellow onions, chopped

2 bay leaves

2 sprigs fresh thyme

1 medium can beans (save bean sauce)

2 (6-ounce) ham hocks

5 cups Ham Hock Broth (recipe on page 160)

2 pounds pork shoulder, bone-in

1 teaspoon butter

4 (12-ounce) pork chops

salt and pepper

fresh thyme

olive oil, plus more for greens

mustard greens sprouts, or micro mustard greens

salt and pepper

1 lemon, juiced

Chow-Chow

1 cup distilled white vinegar

½ cup water

½ cup sugar

2 sprigs thyme

1 bay leaf

1 red bell pepper, finely diced

(continued on page 160)

Preheat oven to 375 degrees F.

In a large pot add olive oil, bacon, fatback, onions, bay leaves, thyme, beans and ham hocks. Add Ham Hock Broth and turn burner to low. Add slice of pork shoulder to heated beans. Cook until pork is done.

Remove ham hock, bay leaves and pork shoulder.

Strain beans and reserve sauce. Pour bean sauce into a saucepan. Heat on a burner. Add butter. Whisk butter into sauce. Set aside.

Season pork chops with salt, pepper and fresh thyme. Pan roast in an iron skillet with olive oil over medium-low heat. Turn after 6 minutes and cook until done (15 minutes). Bake in oven 8 to 12 minutes.

Mix micro mustard greens with olive oil, salt, pepper and lemon juice.

Spoon about 2 to 3 tablespoons pork and bean mixture onto large plate. Place slice of pork shoulder and a pork chop on plate. Top with Chow-Chow and greens.

Chow-Chow: Combine vinegar, water, sugar, thyme and bay leaf in heavy-bottomed pan. Bring to boil. Taste and adjust to your liking. Add more sugar if you want it sweeter, more vinegar if you like it tart, and more water to make it less tart. Add peppers and onion. Simmer for 15 minutes. Do not drain. Cool in juices. Add parsley and lemon juice. Set aside.

(continued on page 160)

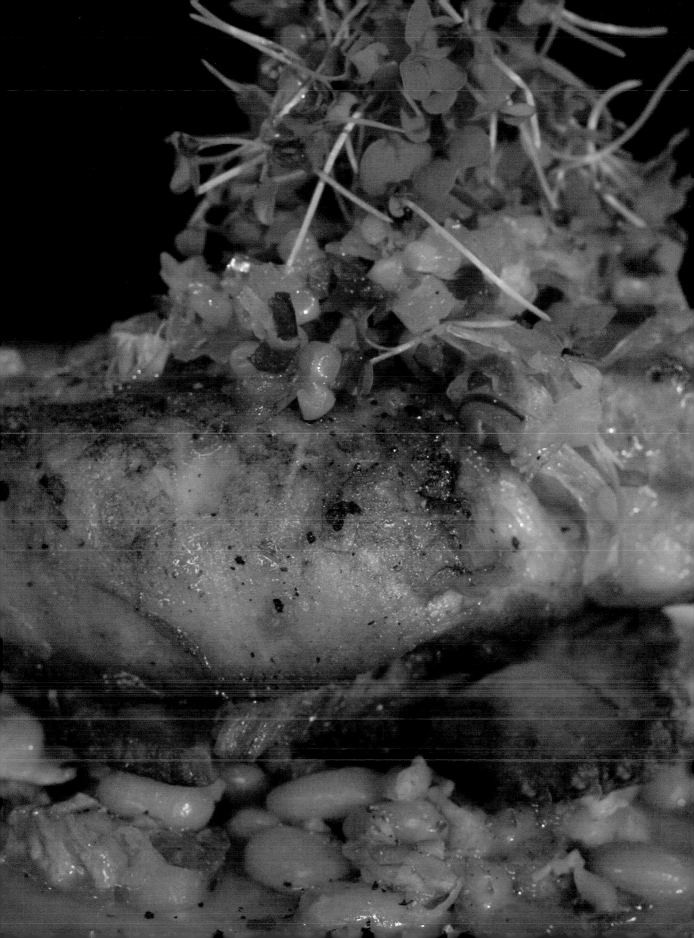

1 yellow pepper, finely diced
1 poblano pepper, finely diced
1 yellow onion, finely diced
2 teaspoons finely chopped parsley
lemon juice

Ham Hock Broth

5 pounds rib, shoulder and neck
   bones from a small pig
3 carrots, roughly chopped
3 stalks celery, roughly chopped
2 yellow onions, roughly chopped
4 cloves garlic, diced
2 bay leaves
4 ham hocks

Makes 4 servings

Thom's Tips: This dish is a pork lover's dream. If the butcher doesn't have the pork shoulder or the ham hock, you can still make the dish. What you will lose on flavor, you will make up by cutting calories.

Ham Hock Broth: Preheat oven to 400 degrees F. Rinse trimmings in cold water. Brown trimmings in oven for 30 minutes. Place the browned trimmings in a large stockpot. Add carrots, celery, onions, garlic, bay leaves and ham hocks. Add water to cover. Simmer for 4 hours. Strain, cool and reserve.

Wine Pairing:
Castelmaure — 'Clos des Vents' Corbieres

Aris's Wine Notes: This is a hearty dish needing a wine of equal stature. The Languedoc region in France delivers some of the best values in robust red wines. This is a fat, ripe and juicy wine with the spicy, roasted quality to the fruit that one finds in southern Rhone Valley wines. The pork actually enhances the flavors of the wine, while the wine provides a firm, palate-cleansing structure, to the benefit of both.

Underwood
Pork Chop

From: Pewter Rose Bistro • 1820 South Boulevard • Charlotte, NC 28203

Start your grill.

Steep lavender in water for 15 to 30 minutes. Combine lavender water with honey, vinegar, olive oil, salt and pepper; cool marinade.

Place pork chops in a zip-lock bag with marinade. Allow to marinate 30 minutes at room temperature or up to 1 day refrigerated.

Coat melon wedges with olive oil. Grill on hot grill until warm and grill marks form. Set aside and keep warm.

Pour vinegar in a saucepan and reduce over medium-high heat until syrup consistency.

Remove chops from marinade. Spray with nonstick pan coating. Grill until just pink, approximately 3 to 5 minutes per side. Place rice, chop and melon on plate. Drizzle with reduced balsamic syrup.

Shallot Rice:

Sauté shallot in olive oil until lightly browned. Add shallot to rice and salt. Follow rice cooker procedure (15 minutes) or cook on stove for 20 minutes with 2 ¼ cups water.

Wine Pairing:
La Puerta — Malbec

Aris's Wine Notes: Malbec has become the signature red grape of Argentina. La Puerta's is on the tamer side of the Malbec spectrum, but retains plenty of power for this dish. It's similar to Cabernet Sauvignon in its concentrated flavors and chewy, tannic structure, but the flavor profile is quite different. There is a meaty texture to the wine that matches the marvelous texture of the pork chop to a tee.

1 cup lavender, dry
1 cup water
12 ounces honey
2 cups balsamic vinegar
1 cup olive oil
salt and pepper
4 pork chops
1 cantaloupe, peeled and cut in wedges
extra virgin olive oil
1 cup balsamic vinegar
non-stick spray

Shallot Rice

1 shallot bulb, peeled
1 tablespoon olive oil
2 cups jasmine rice
1 tablespoon kosher salt
water

Makes 4 servings

Thom's Tips: An easy way to marinate your meat is to fill a zip-lock bag with the marinade and place the meat inside. After zipping it up, just put it in the refrigerator for a day. There's no mess, no lids to knock off and no dishes to clean.

Grilled Linguiça
with Four Cheese Polenta, Grilled Vegetables & Tomato Fondue

From: The Plantation Room at Celebration Hotel • 700 Bloom Street • Celebration, FL 34747

2 quarts chicken stock or canned chicken broth

2½ cups polenta

¼ cup grated Parmesan cheese, plus extra for garnish

¼ cup grated mozzarella cheese

¼ cup grated Romano cheese

¼ cup grated white cheddar cheese

6 small portobello mushroom caps, peeled

1 yellow squash, sliced

1 zucchini, sliced

4 linguiça sausages, grilled

½ cup olive oil

4 tablespoons minced garlic

¼ cup white wine

8 Roma tomatoes, chopped

5 basil leaves

1 cup water

salt and pepper to taste

Makes 4 to 6 servings

Thom's Tips: The four cheese polenta also makes a great breakfast food. You can heat it in a sauté pan with a little oil or butter and serve with preserves.

Start your grill.

Preheat oven to 350 degrees F.

Bring chicken stock to a boil in a medium saucepan. Add polenta and stir often. Cook the polenta over low heat and add all of the cheeses. Stir constantly. Cook on low for 12 minutes or until thick like grits. Pour the mixture onto a shallow baking pan and put it in the freezer.

Grill the mushrooms, vegetables and sausage.

In a small saucepan heat oil and garlic, but do not brown the garlic. Add wine to the pot, then the tomatoes. Add basil and blend the sauce slightly. Add water and return to low heat for 10 minutes. Add salt and pepper to taste.

When polenta is firm to the touch use a 4-inch circle cutter to cut the polenta. Place the polenta circles in the oven until slightly brown.

Plate by stacking the polenta on top of the tomato fondue, followed by the grilled vegetables and sausage. Garnish with grated Parmesan cheese.

Wine Pairing:
Oyster Bay — Pinot Noir

Aris's Wine Notes: Ripe cherry and plum-like fruit with notes of new leather blend effortlessly with the cheese, while lightly toasty oak, previously hidden behind the fruit, comes into action to play off against the smoky taste in the sausage. The creaminess of the polenta matches the plush texture of the wine, while the wine's underlying acidity firms up the finish and ties the package together. I love it when a match comes together like this.

Coffee-Rubbed Pork Tenderloin
with Vegetable Risotto

From: Hadco Facility • 101 West Worthington Avenue • Charlotte, NC 28203

Risotto

4 cups unsalted chicken broth

2 tablespoons extra virgin olive oil

3 shallots, finely diced

¼ cup celery, small dice

2 cups risotto

½ cup dry white wine

1 cup zucchini, small dice

1 cup carrot, small dice

3 stalks asparagus, small dice

½ cup unsalted butter

grated Parmesan Reggiano

kosher salt

white pepper

Pork Tenderloin

2 pounds pork tenderloin

1 tablespoon espresso granules

¼ teaspoon kosher salt

½ teaspoon ground cumin

1 teaspoon ground coriander

1 teaspoon cardamom

1 teaspoon cayenne pepper

1 large clove garlic, minced

1 tablespoon minced fresh ginger

1 teaspoon lemon zest

1 tablespoon olive oil

cilantro, garnish

Makes 4 servings

Preheat oven to 350 degrees F.

Risotto:

Heat chicken broth in a pot over medium heat.

In a saucepan, heat olive oil. Add the shallots and celery. Cook it down for a minute or so and then add risotto to pan and toast for about 1 minute. Add wine to the pan and let alcohol evaporate. Add vegetables and a little broth and cook. Ladle by ladle, add the broth to the risotto, stirring every so often to keep the risotto from sticking to the bottom of the pan, but not too often; you do not want to "polish" the grain. When al dente, add butter and cheese. Season with salt and pepper.

Pork Tenderloin:

Wash your pork tenderloin with cold water and dry it thoroughly. Trim any fat on the outside of the pork.

Mix together espresso granules, salt, cumin, coriander, cardamom, cayenne, garlic, ginger, lemon zest and olive oil. The consistency should be "pasty." Rub the paste all over the tenderloin.

Cook in oven for 20 minutes or until meat thermometer reads 145 degrees. Remove from oven and let rest. The thermometer should read 155 to 160 degrees, a safe temperature for pork.

Spoon risotto onto plate. Top with three slices of pork. Garnish with cilantro.

<u>Wine Pairing:</u>
Banfi — Centine

Aris's Wine Notes: This American-owned estate has been declared "Italy's Best Wine Estate" eleven times since 1994 at VinItaly. Centine is a blend of 60% Sangiovese, 20 percent Cabernet Sauvignon and 20 per-cent Merlot. The combination of grapes creates enough weight and struc-ture in the wine to handle the pork without overwhelming it. The spice and tobacco nuances of Sangiovese work well with most of the dish's components, but the coffee required the extra richness of the Cabernet and Merlot.

Thom's Tips: You don't want to stir risotto too often. If you continually stir the risotto as it is cooking it will separate the starch from the rice as it absorbs the water, causing the rice to "polish." On the other hand, if you don't stir at all, you'll need a jackhammer to get it out of the pot. The method I learned was one stir per every 2 ladles of liquid.

Pork Chop
Alla Zingara

From: La Cava Restaurant • 329 South Church Street • Salisbury, NC 28144

4 center-cut pork chops with two
    bones
salt and pepper
2 tablespoons olive oil
1 medium zucchini, julienned (by
    mandolin)
2 tablespoons butter
6 sun-dried tomatoes, julienned
4 thick slices prosciutto, julienned
4 marinated artichokes, quartered
¼ cup white wine
6 mushrooms, sliced
cracked black pepper, to taste
¾ cup brown sauce or demi-glace

Makes 4 servings

Thom's Tips: Pork, the other white meat, is fully cooked when it is white in the middle.

Preheat oven to 450 degrees F.

Season pork chops with salt and pepper. Pan sear on both sides in hot oil until brown. Bake them in the oven for 8 minutes; turn after 4 minutes.

While the pork chops are cooking, sauté the zucchini with half of the butter for 1 minute. Drain the liquid. Add the sun-dried tomatoes and cook for 30 seconds.

Remove the pork chops from the oven, take them out of the pan and place them in a dish to rest.

Drain the excess oil from the pan. Add the prosciutto and the artichokes to the hot pan and cook on top of the stove for 20 to 30 seconds. Deglaze the pan with wine, add mushrooms, cracked black pepper and reduce for another 1 to 2 minutes. Add the brown sauce, and remaining butter, and reduce until thick.

Mound the zucchini and sun-dried tomatoes in the center of the plates, lay the pork chops on top of it and cover with the sauce.

Wine Pairing:
Garetto — Barbera D'Asti

Aris's Wine Notes: This Barbera is a deliciously fruity and supple wine whose tasty ripeness, refreshing acidity and friendly character allow it to fit in nicely with many dishes and occasions. Pork pairs well with red wines that focus on natural fruitiness and do not have noticeable oak flavors. Pork is also rich enough to need the balancing effect of acidity and Barbera is happy to oblige.

Desserts

Blackberry Confit
with Peppermint and Honey Whipped Cream

From: Inn on Biltmore Estate • 1 Approach Road • Asheville, NC 28803

½ cup sugar

½ cup water

1 vanilla bean, split

1 cup blackberries

peppermint leaves

1 cup heavy whipping cream

1 cup honey

Makes 4 servings

Thom's Tips: You don't need a fancy, smancy pastry bag. All you need is a lowly zip-lock bag. Just fill it up with whatever ingredient you want to pipe onto your dish. Cut a small hole in one corner, then squeeze.

In a small saucepan, combine sugar and water. Bring to a boil, then turn down to medium heat. Add the vanilla bean and simmer for 3 to 4 minutes. Remove from heat. Remove vanilla bean. Pour directly over the blackberries.

Cut peppermint in thin strips and add to the blackberries.

Whip the heavy cream to stiff peaks and fold in the honey.

Ladle blackberries onto plate. Top with whipped cream. Garnish with extra mint.

Wine Pairing:
Biltmore Estate —— Century White

Aris's Wine Notes: What an interesting blend of grapes. The Riesling offers floral aromas and citrus fruits and the Muscat adds tropical fruits while the Gewurztraminer chimes in with roses and lychee. The wine is on the delicate side and only mildly sweet, which is just fine here because this dessert is not very sweet and already has acidity from the blackberries.

Vanilla Creams
with Fresh Berries

From: Fenwick's On Providence • **511 Providence Road** • **Charlotte, NC 28207**

8 ounces cream cheese, softened

2 cups heavy cream

1 cup sour cream

¾ cup sugar

1 envelope unflavored gelatin

¼ cup warm water

1 cup blueberries

1 cup sliced strawberries

1 cup blackberries

1 peach, sliced

¼ cup sugar

Strawberry Sauce

1 pint strawberries

¼ cup sugar

1 ounce rum

¼ cup pineapple juice

Make 4 to 6 servings

Thom's Tips: When picking a wine to go with a dessert, Aris has taught me a wonderful tip. The dessert wine should be sweeter than the dessert. While any wine rule can always be broken, especially when serving chocolate or foolishly considering malt liquor, it's a good rule of thumb.

In a freestanding countertop mixer, whip the cream cheese until it looks like frosting.

In a saucepan, gently heat the cream, sour cream and sugar until mixture is hot and sugar is melted. Remove from heat.

Dissolve gelatin in the warm water. Pour into the cream mixture and mix together. Add cream and gelatin mixture to cream cheese and whip on low for about 5 minutes, or until cream cheese is completely dissolved. Pour into either a well-oiled mold or individual serving glasses and chill. (Can chill for up to 48 hours).

Combine blueberries, strawberries, blackberries and peach with sugar. Set aside.

Just before serving, unmold. Top with fresh sugared fruit and Strawberry Sauce.

Strawberry Sauce:

Purée strawberries, sugar, rum and pineapple juice in blender. Set aside.

<u>Wine Pairing:</u>
Robert Mondavi — Moscato d'Oro

Aris's Wine Notes: With such a sinfully sweet and luscious wine paired with a decadently rich dessert, why bother with the main course? Actually, the main course does serve to suppress your appetite enough so you don't go totally overboard; relying on will power is futile. The vanilla cream adds another dimension of flavor and richness, while the acidity in the fresh berries helps cleanse the palate.

Turtle Kraals
Mud Pie

From: Key West Grill • 1214 Celebrity Circle # R7 • Myrtle Beach, SC 29577

In a springform pan, line the bottom of the pan with crushed and crumbled chocolate chip cookies. Spoon first layer of ice cream and make small rounded lumps. Drizzle hot fudge on top of ice cream. Let fudge fall randomly into the crevices of the ice cream. Spoon on second layer of ice cream. Finish with drizzled hot fudge and more cookie crumbs. Freeze.

Serve with whipped cream and cherries.

Wine Pairing:

Mionetto — Moscato della Venezia

Aris's Wine Notes: Anyone who has not tried an Italian Moscato is missing out on one of the most delightful, fun-loving and reasonably priced dessert wines you'll find anywhere. Its low alcohol and light carbonation yields a soft, creamy palate, which accentuates its sweetness and carries the delightful tropical fruit flavors to every corner of the palate. The fine "scrubbing bubbles" refresh the palate, allowing the wine to act like an exotic fruit topping for the pie.

1 package chocolate chip cookies, crumbled
1 gallon coffee ice cream, thawed
hot fudge
1 can whipped cream
maraschino cherries

Makes 6 to 8 servings

Thom's Tips: Want to avoid spending more time cleaning up from your mixing than you did using the mixer? Wrap saran wrap around the bowl and over the top of the mixer. That way you can turn it on high speed without making a mess.

Raspberry Soufflé
with Whipped Cream

From: Grape Escape • **62 North Lexington** • **Asheville, NC 28801**

8 egg whites

⅓ cup water

1 cup sugar

1 cup raspberries

1 tablespoon soft or melted butter

¼ cup sugar

vanilla ice cream

Makes 4 to 6 servings

Thom's Tips: Quick vanilla sauce recipe. Take your favorite vanilla ice cream and melt on the stove over low heat.

Preheat oven to 400 degrees F.

Whip egg whites to a firm texture. In a saucepan, over medium-high heat, combine water, sugar and raspberries. Cook to a soft ball or 240 degrees. On low speed, slowly add syrup to egg whites. Don't overmix.

In advance, lightly brush the inside of each soufflé bowl with the soft or melted butter. Sugar the inside of each bowl and keep in a cool area.

Fill each bowl with the soufflé base and tap the bottom with your hand.

Cook for 8 to 10 minutes, or until the soufflés hold firm when you shake the oven rack.

Serve immediately with vanilla ice cream. You can also garnish with whipped cream or vanilla sauce.

Wine Pairing:
Robert Mondavi —— Moscato d'Oro

Aris's Wine Notes: A seductive floral perfume of honeysuckle and lusciously sweet palate loaded with tropical fruit, ripe peach and citrus makes it a delight to both nose and palate. Pairing this with a raspberry dessert proves to be a great match. The raspberry provides a needed dose of tartness to help cut through the sweetness and rich cream.

Caribbean "Bananas Foster" with Toasted Coconut-Rum Ice Cream

From: The Speedway Club • Lowe's Motor Speedway • PO Box 600 • Concord, NC 28027

1¾ cups butter, divided

6 sheets phyllo dough

4 bananas, peeled

¼ cup brown sugar

1¾ cups heavy cream

2¼ cups granulated sugar

2 cups water

1 cup dark rum

mint sprig

Toasted Coconut-Rum Ice Cream

4 cups Cocoa Lopez

2¾ cups milk

¼ cup rum

3 tablespoons toasted coconut flakes

Makes 4 servings

Preheat oven to 350 degrees F.

Melt 1 cup of butter. Brush each phyllo sheet with melted butter. Layer three sheets on top of one another. Cut the phyllo dough in half. Slice a peeled banana on each half. Pack brown sugar on the banana and roll up. Tuck the ends under and brush the outside of the dough with melted butter. Place on a half sheet pan and bake until light brown and crispy.

While the banana is baking, combine the cream and remaining butter in a saucepan and cook over medium heat until the butter is melted and the mixture comes to a simmer. Remove from the heat. In another saucepan, combine the sugar and water and cook over high heat to a medium-dark caramel, washing down the sides of the pan as necessary to prevent crystals from forming. Remove the pan from the heat and, while stirring constantly, slowly and carefully pour the warm cream mixture into the caramel. Cool slightly and stir in the dark rum. Cool completely.

When the bananas are cooked, remove from the oven and slice in half on an angle. Rest one half on top of the other and place a large scoop of Toasted Coconut-Rum Ice Cream in the middle. Pour the caramel rum sauce over the ice cream, garnish with a mint sprig and serve at once.

Toasted Coconut-Rum Ice Cream:

Combine Cocoa Lopez, milk and rum in a large bowl and whisk till blended. Chill and add toasted coconut. Process in an ice cream machine according to the manufacturer's instructions.

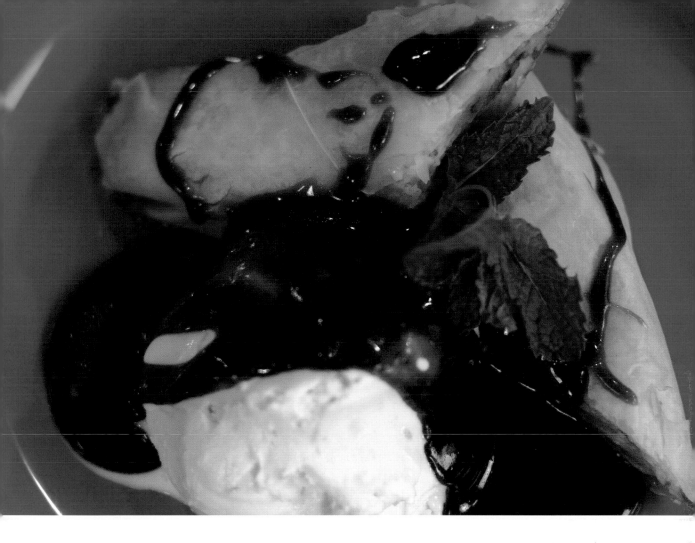

Wine Pairing:
Duplin — Scuppernong

Aris's Wine Notes: Duplin is the oldest and largest winery in the Southeast. Scuppernong is the oldest and most famous variety of the grape species commonly called Muscadine. These Scuppernong wines can taste quite pungent and exotic. The flavors are overtly fruity and have a unique pungent flavor often described as "foxy." All of the flavors in the wine and the dessert magically work together for a satisfying and interesting match.

Thom's Tips: Between the TV crew and myself we managed to go through an entire can of Cocoa Lopez on the set. We experimented with it in recipes for syrup, ice cream and gluing random objects to the counter. Mixed with pineapple, ice and rum, it makes the best piña coladas I've ever had. Ramon Lopez Irizarry, a professor at the University of Puerto Rico, originally invented Cocoa Lopez through a government grant. The sweet, half coconut, half cane sugar syrup is truly a wonderful concoction.

Banana Rama

From: Key West Grill • **1214 Celebrity Circle # R7** • **Myrtle Beach, SC 29577**

4 bananas

1 cup egg wash (two eggs and 1
 cup milk)

2 cups shredded coconut

2 cups Total cereal, crushed

vegetable oil

½ gallon vanilla ice cream

Grand Marnier

1 can whipped cream

chocolate syrup

maraschino cherries

mint leaves

Makes 4 servings

Thom's Tips: On the set, we discovered a recipe for one the best piña coladas we have ever had: ⅓ cup pineapple juice, ¼ cup Cocoa Lopez, ¾ cup ice, ⅓ cup rum. Put in a bender. Blend and serve.

Peel bananas and then dip in egg wash. Roll bananas in coconut and then dip in egg wash again. Roll bananas in crushed cereal. Deep-fry encrusted bananas for about 2 minutes, or until golden brown.

Top with ice cream and Grand Marnier. Garnish with whipped cream, chocolate syrup, cherries and mint leaves.

Wine Pairing:
Mionetto — Moscato della Venezia

Aris's Wine Notes: Anyone who has not tried an Italian Moscato is missing out on one of the most delightful, fun-loving and reasonably priced dessert wines you'll find anywhere. Its low alcohol and light carbonation yields a soft, creamy palate, which accentuates its sweetness and carries the delightful tropical fruit flavors to every corner of the palate. The fine "scrubbing bubbles" refresh the palate, allowing the wine to act like an exotic fruit topping for the pie.

Bananas Foster Crêpes

From: 700 Drayton—Mansion on Forsyth Park • 700 Drayton Street • Savannah, GA 31401

In a mixing bowl, combine eggs, milk, water, flour, melted butter, sugar and vanilla, and liqueur if using; whisk well. Place the batter in the refrigerator for 1 hour. This allows the bubbles to subside. Batter will hold up to 48 hours.

Heat a small non-stick pan. Add butter to coat pan. Pour ¼ cup of batter in the center of the pan and then swirl to spread evenly. Cook for approximately 30 seconds and flip. Cook for another 10 seconds. Remove and lay flat; allow to cool. After cooling, the crêpes can be stacked with wax paper between the layers.

Sweet Crêpe Topping:

Slice banana. In sauté pan, melt butter and brown sugar. Add spiced rum and then bananas. Fold crêpes into quarters. Place in a sauté pan with sauce and bananas. Allow sauce to soak into crêpes. Remove from pan and plate. Garnish with powdered sugar.

Wine Pairing:
Chateau Rieussec — Sauternes

Aris's Wine Notes: Chateau Rieussec is one of the world's great wines, an incredibly luscious dessert wine whose flavors of ripe figs, tropical fruits and citrus zest combined with honey and apricot notes is exquisite. The best any dessert can do with a superstar like Rieussec is to be a great supporting actor, and these Bananas Foster Crêpes do an admirable job.

2 large eggs
¾ cup milk
½ cup water
1 cup flour
3 tablespoons melted butter
2½ tablespoons sugar
1 teaspoon vanilla
2 tablespoons of your favorite
    liqueur, optional
butter

Sweet Crêpe Topping

1 banana
2 tablespoons butter
½ cup brown sugar
spiced rum
powdered sugar

Makes 4 to 6 servings

Thom's Tips: Make your own vanilla. Take a bottle of any plain liquor. Cut open a vanilla bean. Scrape the vanilla seeds. Add the seeds and the cut vanilla bean to the liquor. Store in the cabinet and use as vanilla extract.

Molten Chocolate Cake
with Godiva Hot Fudge Sauce

From: Motor Supply Company Bistro • **920 Gervais Street** • **Columbia, SC 29209**

1 pound bittersweet chocolate

1 pound butter

8 whole eggs

8 yolks

¾ cup sugar

1 tablespoon vanilla extract

8 tablespoons all-purpose flour

1 teaspoon salt

Godiva Hot Fudge Sauce

½ cup heavy cream

⅓ cup chocolate liquor

½ cup sugar

½ teaspoon fine salt

½ teaspoon vanilla extract

4 to 5 cups Godiva dark chocolate chips

3½ tablespoons butter

Makes 6 servings

Thom's Tips: In my kitchen, I don't have a fancy double boiler. Instead, I use the home-made version. First, I place a large pot on the stove and fill about ⅔ of it with boiling water. Then, I take a smaller soup pot with a long handle and float it on the boiling water in the larger pot. The ingredients, like chocolate, that I don't want to scorch with direct heat, go in the soup pot and are gently heated with the boiling water.

Preheat oven to 400 degrees F.

Gently melt chocolate and butter together in double boiler over medium heat. Beat together the whole eggs, yolks, sugar and vanilla. Add the flour and salt. Now beat the melted chocolate and butter with the eggs and sugar. Place in small buttered molds and bake for 7 minutes.

Godiva Hot Fudge Sauce:

In a saucepan, combine heavy cream, chocolate liquor, sugar, salt and vanilla extract. Bring to a boil. Slowly stir in the chocolate and butter until smooth.

Allow cakes to cool enough to remove molds. Ladle fudge sauce over cakes.

<u>Wine Pairing:</u>
Mia's Playground — Old Vine Zinfandel

Aris's Wine Notes: Dark purple in color, this old-vine Zinfandel has a nose layered with jammy fruit, white pepper, licorice and vanilla. Old Vine Zin is one of the few table wines that can do dual service with dessert. The super-ripe, jammy fruit combine with soft tannins and high alcohol to give the wine a sense of sweetness and port-like richness that goes quite well with chocolate.

Flaky Apple Tart
with Caramel Sauce and Vanilla Ice Cream

From: 95 Cordova • 95 Cordova Street • St. Augustine, FL 32084

4 apples, peeled and sliced

2 tablespoons unsalted butter

4 tablespoons brown sugar

½ cup raisins and golden raisins

Grand Marnier or other liquor for
    flambé

2 tablespoons orange juice

¾ cup sugar

2 tablespoons water

1 cup heavy cream

2 egg yolks

6 squares of puff pastry, 5 x 5-inch
    or smaller

vanilla ice cream

Makes 6 servings

Thom's Tips: Today's word is flambé. It is a French term for a technique where alcohol is added to the ingredients in a hot pan to create a burst of flames. It is recommended to use an 80 proof or higher alcohol. Some think that the flames change the chemistry of the food, but I just love to release my inner pyro and watch the flames of the alcohol fire.

Preheat oven to 400 degrees F.

Sauté apples in butter with sugar and raisins. Cook until lightly soft. Add Grand Marnier. If cooking with gas, allow the apple mixture to catch fire. When flame dies back, add a splash of orange juice; let cool.

In a saucepan, melt sugar until caramelized. Add water and simmer until soft. Add cream and egg yolks. Cook until back of spoon coats. Keep at room temperature.

Put apple mix on puff pastries, in the centers. Bake for 10 minutes or until golden brown.

Set on plate. Finish with caramel sauce and vanilla ice cream.

Wine Pairing:
Pride Mountain — Viognier

Aris's Wine Notes: The tried and true rule for desserts is to pair with a wine sweeter than the dessert. The plan here was to pair a dry wine with dessert, hoping the richness of its fruit would be enough to balance the sweetness of the dessert. Sometimes you can break the rules and sometimes they break you.

Tiramisu

From: Hadco Facility • 101 West Worthington Avenue • Charlotte, NC 28203

8 eggs

¾ cup sugar

2 cups mascarpone cheese

1 tablespoon Marsala (optional)

8 ounces Savoiardi (ladyfingers)
    biscuits

1½ cups coffee

2 tablespoons cocoa powder

Makes 6 to 8 servings

Thom's Tips: Quality of coffee makes a huge difference in this recipe. You can use instant coffee if you have to, but I am a big fan of using espresso on the biscuits.

Separate the eggs and beat the whites until stiff, then place in the refrigerator. Beat the yolks together with the sugar, then add the mascarpone (also add Marsala here if you choose). Mix well, then add the egg whites.

Dip the biscuits in the coffee and place a single layer in a pan and cover with half of the mascarpone cream. Add another layer of biscuits and top with the remaining mascarpone mixture. Sprinkle the top with cocoa powder and refrigerate for at least 4 hours before serving.

Beer Pairing:
Young's — Double Chocolate Stout

Aris's Beer Notes: Beer with dessert is not common, but it works perfectly here. Young's Double Chocolate Stout is made with real dark chocolate that complements and balances the roast coffee nuances of the dark roasted malted barley. These same flavors are present in the dessert, but are altered by the cheese and Marsala. Not only do all the flavors marry together well, but the beer effervescence cuts through the dessert's richness.

Mucho
Berry

From: The Prickly Pear • 761 North Main Street • Mooresville, NC 28115

8 sheets phyllo dough

2 tablespoons butter, melted

½ cup sliced strawberries

½ cup blackberries

½ cup blueberries

½ cup raspberries

1 teaspoon chambord or raspberry
   liquor

1 teaspoon grenadine

1 teaspoon tequila

¼ cup water

2 tablespoons confectioners' sugar

2 teaspoons lemon peel, divided

1 cup heavy cream

1 lemon, juiced

Makes 4 servings

Thom's Tips: Phyllo dough is fun to work with, but dries out very quickly. Once the dough is dry, it becomes very brittle and just about useless. When working with phyllo dough, take a slightly damp dish cloth and place it over the dough to keep the dough moist.

Preheat oven to 400 degrees F.

Place the 8 sheets of phyllo dough on a baking sheet on top of each other. Brush each sheet with melted butter, thoroughly covering the sheets. Slice the dough in quarters and then diagonally. Set timer for 5 minutes and place phyllo dough in oven.

Combine berries in a bowl. Add chambord, grenadine, tequila and water. Stir in 1 tablespoon confectioners' sugar. Add 1 teaspoon lemon peel. Let stand for 10 minutes.

Pour heavy cream into a bowl and whip until it has soft peaks. Add juice from 1 lemon. Add remaining sugar. Whip to stiff peaks.

To plate the dish, place a good sized dollop of whipped cream in the middle of a plate. Place a phyllo dough triangle over the cream and top with a tablespoonful of berries. Repeat twice. Top off plate with lemon peel and confectioners' sugar.

Wine Pairing:
Mionetto —— Il Rosso

Aris's Wine Notes: Boy, did I get it right this time on the pairing! Mucho berries in the dish, mucho berries in the wine and mucho bubbles to cleanse the palate. This delightful and zesty red sparkling wine comes from the Veneto region in northern Italy. It is not as effervescent as a typical sparkling wine, allowing it to portray a softer, easy going personality.

Resources

Recipes that appear in this book are from the following restaurants:

45 South (pages 40, 73, 150)
20 East Broad Street
Savannah, GA 31401
www.thepirateshouse.com

95 Cordova (pages 115, 180)
95 Cordova Street
St. Augustine, FL 32084
904-810-6810; www.95cordova.com

700 Cooking School—Mansion on Forsyth Park (pages 46, 110, 122)
700 Drayton Street
Savannah, GA 31401
888-711-5114; mansiononforsythpark.com

700 Drayton—Mansion on Forsyth Park (pages 23, 35, 88, 177)
700 Drayton Street
Savannah, GA 31401
888-711-5114; mansiononforsythpark.com

Angus Barn Restaurant (pages 132, 134)
9401 Glenwood Avenue
Raleigh, NC 27617
919-781-2444; www.angusbarn.com

Arpa—Spanish Wine Bar/Tapas Bar (page 104)
121 West Trade Street
Charlotte, NC 28202
704-372-7793; www.arpagrill.com

Bovine's Wood Fired Grill (page 140)
3979 Hwy 17 Business
Murrells Inlet, SC 29576
843-651-2888; www.divinedininggroup.com

Cafe on the Square (pages 72, 108, 118)
One Biltmore Avenue
Asheville, NC 28801
828-251-5565; www.cafeonthesquare.com

Cajun Queen (pages 71, 99, 119)
1800 E 7th Street
Charlotte, NC 28204
704-377-9017; www.cajunqueenrestaurant.net

Chelsea's Wine Bar & Eatery (pages 25, 32, 112)
One South Front Street
Wilmington, NC 28401
910-763-8463; www.chelseasdowntown.com

Christopher's New Global Cuisine (pages 68, 85, 92)
712 Brookstown Ave
Winston-Salem, NC 27101
336-724-1395; www.christophersngc.com

City Tavern Hearst Tower (pages 69, 116, 154)
215 South Tryon, Suite D
Charlotte, NC 28202
704-334-6688; www.city-tavern.com

Crescent Grill (pages 38, 84, 107)
1053 Broad Street
Camden, SC 29020
803-713-0631

Divine Dining Group (pages 96, 102)
3993 Hwy 17
Murrells Inlet, SC 29576
800-365-1773; www.divinedininggroup.com

Fenwick's On Providence (pages 22, 135, 170)
511 Providence Road
Charlotte, NC 28207
704-333-2750

Four Square Restaurant (pages 14, 78, 94)
2701 Chapel Hill Road
Durham, NC 27707
919-401-9877; www.foursquarerestaurant.com

Frazier's Bistro (pages 58, 74)
2418 Hillsborough Street
Raleigh, NC 27607
919-828-6699; www.fraziersbistro.com

Gervais and Vine (pages 34, 156, 157)
620-A Gervais Street
Columbia, SC 29201
803-799-8463; www.gervine.com

Gianni & Gaitano's (pages 24, 36, 70)
14460-171 New Falls of the Neuse Road
Raleigh, NC 27614
919-256-8100
www.gianniandgaitanos.com

Grape Escape (pages 86, 172)
62 North Lexington
Asheville, NC 28801
828-350-1140; www.ashevillegrapeescape.com

Hadco Facility (pages 164, 182)
101 West Worthington Avenue
Charlotte, NC 28203
704-332-0909; www.hadco.net

Inn at Brevard (pages 100, 139)
410 East Main Street
Brevard, NC 28712
828-884-2105; www.theinnatbrevard.com

Inn on Biltmore Estate (pages 16, 60, 66, 90, 168)
1 Approach Road
Asheville, NC 28803
800-624-1575;
biltmore.com/explore/inn/inn.shtml

Jujube Restaurant—Asian Kitchen and Bar
(pages 20, 120, 144)
1201-L Raleigh Road
Chapel Hill, NC 27514
919-960-0555; www.jujuberestaurant.com

Key West Grill (pages 81, 171, 176)
1214 Celebrity Circle # R7
Myrtle Beach, SC 29577
843-444-3663; www.keywestgrill.net

La Cava Restaurant (pages 17, 77, 145, 166)
329 South Church Street
Salisbury, NC 28144
704-637-7174; www.lacavarestaurant.com

Made in Japan Catering (pages 50, 52, 54)
PO Box 240724
Charlotte, NC 28224-0724
704-578-1952; www.madeinjapancatering.com

Mangia Mangia (pages 39, 129, 142)
100 State Street
Columbia, SC 29169
803-791-3443

Mia Famiglia (pages 56, 80, 124)
19918 North Cove Road
Cornelius, NC 28031
704-987-3877; www.miafam.com

Mimosa Grill (page 158)
327 South Tryon Street
Charlotte, NC 28202
704-343-0700; www.mimosagrill.com

Motor Supply Company Bistro (pages 44, 128, 178)
920 Gervais Street
Columbia, SC 29209
(803) 256-6687; www.motorsupplybistro.com

Mr. Friendly's New Southern Cafe (page 106)
2001-A Greene Street
Columbia, SC 29205
803-254-7828; www.mrfriendlys.com

North Beach Grill (page 48)
Tybee Island, GA 31328
912-786-9003; www.georgesoftybee.com

Pewter Rose Bistro (pages 42, 161)
1820 South Boulevard
Charlotte, NC 28203
704-332-8149; pewterose.com

The Plantation Room at Celebration Hotel
(pages 114, 138, 162)
700 Bloom Street
Celebration, FL 34747
888-499-3800; celebrationhotel.com

The Prickly Pear (pages 28, 146, 184)
761 North Main Street
Mooresville, NC 28115
704-799-0875; www.pricklypear.net

Red Rocks Café (pages 76, 97, 143)
4223-8 Providence Road
Charlotte, NC 28211
704-364-0402; www.redrockscafe.com

Salsa Mexican Caribbean Restaurant (pages
126, 148)
6 Patton Avenue
Asheville, NC 28801
828-252-9805

Salty Caper (pages 62, 64)
115 South Lee Street
Salisbury, NC 28144
704-633-1101; www.saltycaper.com

San Francisco Oven (pages 30, 43)
7223 North Kings Highway
Myrtle Beach, SC 29572
843-692-9780; sanfranciscooven.com

Solstice Kitchen and Wine Bar (pages 91, 136)
841-4 Sparkleberry Lane
Columbia, SC 29229
803-788-6966; www.solsticekitchen.com

The Speedway Club (pages 18, 152, 174)
Lowe's Motor Speedway
PO Box 600
Concord, NC 28027
704-455-3216; www.gospeedwayclub.com

Villa Romana (pages 82, 130, 153)
707 South Kings Hwy
Myrtle Beach, SC 29577
843-448-4990;
www.villaromanamyrtlebeach.com

Vinnie's Steakhouse & Seafood (pages 26,
98, 151)
7440 Six Forks Road
Raleigh, NC 27615
919- 847-7319; www.vinniessteakhouse.com

Index

Metric Conversion Chart

Liquid and Dry Measures

U.S.	Canadian	Australian
¼ teaspoon	1 mL	1 ml
½ teaspoon	2 mL	2 ml
1 teaspoon	5 mL	5 ml
1 Tablespoon	15 mL	20 ml
¼ cup	50 mL	60 ml
⅓ cup	75 mL	80 ml
½ cup	125 mL	125 ml
⅔ cup	150 mL	170 ml
¾ cup	175 mL	190 ml
1 cup	250 mL	250 ml
1 quart	1 liter	1 litre

Temperature Conversion Chart

Fahrenheit	Celsius
250	120
275	140
300	150
325	160
350	180
375	190
400	200
425	220
450	230
475	240
500	260